Kismet

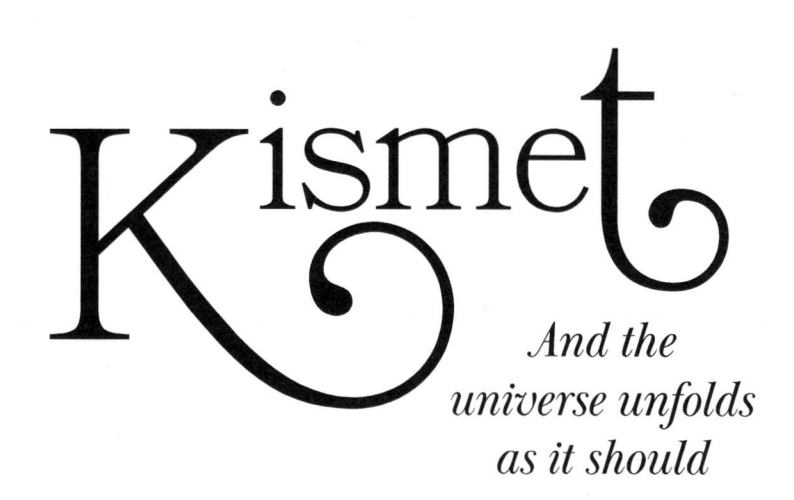

And the universe unfolds as it should

Edith H. Lavroff

◆ FriesenPress

Suite 300 - 990 Fort St
Victoria, BC, V8V 3K2
Canada

www.friesenpress.com

Copyright © 2020 by Edith H. Lavroff
First Edition — 2020

All rights reserved.

www.edithlavroff.com

No part of this publication may be reproduced in any form, or by any means, electronic or mechanical, including photocopying, recording, or any information browsing, storage, or retrieval system, without permission in writing from FriesenPress.

ISBN
978-1-5255-6984-5 (Hardcover)
978-1-5255-6985-2 (Paperback)
978-1-5255-6986-9 (eBook)

1. BIOGRAPHY & AUTOBIOGRAPHY, PERSONAL MEMOIRS

Distributed to the trade by The Ingram Book Company

With love to Wendy!

— Evie

High up in the land called Swithjod,
there stands a rock.
It is a hundred miles high and a hundred
miles wide.
Once every thousand years a little bird comes
to this rock to sharpen its beak.
When the rock has thus been worn away,
then a single day of Eternity
Will have gone by.

From *The Story of Mankind*
by Hendrik Willem van Loon.

PREFACE

When I was 56 years old I found myself having to face the world alone again. I told myself that I would get used to the idea, and that I was a strong and capable woman who would find her way again. I was wrong. When you have a good marriage, you stand back to back, facing the world together. Suddenly, there is no-one to 'have your back'. You are alone. It took two years, but then it caught up with me, and I had what they call a nervous break-down. I could not stop crying and was ready to call it quits.

I had gone back to university to get my degree and was taking five courses. I had to cancel one and had a lot of trouble keeping up with the rest. I was also going to a psychiatric out-patient clinic at the hospital from 9 to 12 four days a week, as per my doctor's orders. At first, I thought *I don't need this. I will get over this on my own. I am not like the others.* I was wrong again. I learned so much there, that I was actually very grateful to my doctor for sending me there. I was trying to get a Bachelor's degree in Psychology so it helped me in that respect too.

I did get my Bachelor's degree, although I had to settle for a B.A. in English Literature with only an extended minor in Psychology. But I was content. Now I looked for some kind of job where I could use my new knowledge. I was over 60 by now and chances of finding anything were remote.

After searching for quite a while I found in Kelowna the Society for Learning in Retirement. It was a charitable institution with a choice of many classes and three semesters per year. Being a history buff, I was happy to see there were some of those classes too. In no time at all, I was leading classes in Ancient Civilizations. I felt free not to stick to a standard view of ancient events, but started asking questions like *could there really have been a historic world-wide flood? Let's find out.* My class and I decided yes there could have been. Or we discussed the Greek myths, and asked ourselves whether they were only just that and nothing more, or whether there could have been some truth to them. And what shape that truth might have taken. There were many more of such subjects we all enjoyed researching and discussing, apart from the usual discussions and lectures on the ancient domains of the world like Sumeria, Babylonia, and Assyria.

My experiences with the Society for Learning in Retirement gave me what I needed. It gave me a reason to look forward to my days, and it forced me to do a lot of research, which I loved. I can never be grateful enough to have had this time in my life. The many friendships that developed have warmed my heart. And there were the many suggestions 'to write my memoirs' all through those sixteen years I was standing in front of those classes. Well, here I am, class. These are the memoirs you asked for. Hope you enjoy reading them!

I want to thank especially some of those friends who read my manuscript, gave suggestions and in general encouraged me in my endeavors. Vera Ito, the president of our society, who was in my classes all along. Vera, it was so good to have your input, ideas, and help all those years. Siggi Narjes, dear friend, your flowers, birthday cards, and birthday celebrations were so much appreciated, as well as your input into my manuscript. Ilse Erwig, who took over my job as Program Chair, and who also lived through horrendous war years in Indonesia, thank you for your support all these years, as well as with my manuscript. It was a lucky day when you joined my classes! Also, thank you Toshi Sakamoto, Linda Grant, and Marvin Mills for all your support and friendship.

An extra special thank you goes out to my dear friend, Ann Cooper, whom I met during my university years. She now lives in England, but we are in constant touch with each other. She read the manuscript and is my most vocal supporter. She also created some of the pictures in my book.

Ingrid Orelov, my beloved cousin from Germany, thanks for reading the manuscript and telling me more about the old days you shared with me. Ingrid now lives in Perth, Australia with her husband.

I also want to thank my entire FriesenPress Team for their support and help during the entire process of getting the book ready for print. You made my life a lot easier than it might have been!

Lastly, I want to thank my wonderful family for being there for me through everything. My son, Michael, my daughter-in-law, Janine, and their four children, Alex, Olivia, Robyn, and Naomi. The first three have given me five terrific great-grandchildren: Jaxon, Norah, Sawyer, Wyatt, and River. Naomi is only fifteen so her time is yet to come.

It rests me only to wish ourselves and the rest of the world a safe end to the dreaded Covid-19 pandemic.

Edie Lavroff, 2020

(Society for Learning in Retirement, 1434 Graham Street, Kelowna, B.C. V1Y 3A8. Phone: 250-448-1203. www.slrkelowna.ca)

CHAPTER ONE

This is all about funny names, beautiful girls, and marriage.

Well, here I am, writing my own biography. Why? Good question. Why do I think I am so important that I need to do this? I am not a movie star, nor a famous politician, nor anything else but a simple housewife. But then, I also believe that every person's life is potentially worthy of a book, because it is not only the adventures we have that make a life interesting, but what goes on inside. It is the struggles we have to accept the situations this life throws at us that make a life interesting.

I was born on a tropical island, was a prisoner of war, lived in exotic places, did things I should not have done, fell deeply in love, and lived every minute of it with great passion. I have a few regrets, but I have many more happy and positive memories. In fact, I'd recommend living another life again. So, here goes!

My dad was a Dutchman, born of Friesian parents. This often means red-headed and stubborn. And the Friesians sure like the ocean and everything that's in it. To illustrate the point, my grandmother's maiden name was Haringa, which means "of the Herring." What do her parents call their little girl? Aaltje Haringa, which means Little Eel of the Herring.

I ask you! And that was not even the worst; her brother was called Haring Haringa, which means Herring of the Herring. To my dad those names sounded perfectly acceptable. He had lots of very Dutch names himself but was soon called "Johnny," which worked for everybody. He left school at sixteen to start working, but when he was eighteen he decided that Holland could not give him what he wanted of life, so he enrolled in the army and was soon sent to Indonesia, which was at that time a colony of the Netherlands. It was 1928. He was looking forward to a stint of six years before he would get six-months leave in Holland.

He spent six busy years on Java and finally managed to go on his first -month furlough. The most pressing item for him now was how to find a girl who would love him enough to follow him to Indonesia. His brother knew the answer. "I will take you to Germany. I know lots of really nice girls there." And Adolf Hitler's rise to power had not impinged enough on either of the brothers at that time, to make them stop and think. It was 1934.

(Hitler was leader of the Nazi Party. He had become Chancellor of Germany in 1933 and became their Führer in 1934).

My dad found the girl he wanted in Germany. She was eighteen, sweet, and very much in love with him. They married on December 29, 1934, and boarded the ship back to Indonesia that very same day. It was the *Christiaan Huygens*.

I was born on August 21, 1935 in Tjimahi (now a suburb of Bandung) on Java.

Those of you who are careful readers will have noticed a slight discrepancy in the date of my birth. They got married on December 29 and I was born on August 21. "Hey, what's with that, mom?" I said later. "Was I born too early?" As I was a bouncing eight-pound, five-ounce baby that did not seem likely, but I had to ask.

My mom hemmed and hawed and blushed, and finally said defensively, "Yes, you were in a hurry to be born."

Yeah right, mom. Well, to speak with the Romans, *Errare humanum est,* which means, of course, that to err is human…

CHAPTER TWO

I plan my arrival in this world very carefully...

It is amazing to me now to realize how little the parents of those days knew about childbirth. My mom and dad were out taking a stroll when she was five-months pregnant, and my dad said to her, "Can't you pull in your stomach a little? Everyone can see that you are pregnant."

I thought that really was the limit of ignorance, but they were well suited, for she said, "No, Johnny, I am trying very hard but it doesn't work."

My date of birth was calculated to be the 31st of August. My dad was always studying for something as he was quite ambitious. On the evening of the 20th of August, he was so occupied when my mom walked in, saying, "Johnny, my stomach hurts so much."

He absentmindedly looked at her and said, "Go take an aspirin, that should take care of it."

"Okay, Johnny," my mom said obediently and went back to their bedroom. A little while later she came back. "Johnny, it really hurts too much; the aspirin is not working. You don't think it could be the baby?"

"No, no, of course not. The baby isn't supposed to be born till the end of the month. Go back to bed and take another aspirin."

"Okay, Johnny," she said again obediently.

For a little while peace reigned in my dad's study, and he happily worked away. Then, suddenly the door was thrown open and my mom cried, "It's the baby, I am sure."

My dad took one look at her and said, "I'll get the midwife immediately. Get back to bed and try not to worry; she'll be here soon to help you."

It wasn't as easy as they hoped it would be. I finally made an appearance at 1.45 p.m. the next day. My dad took one look at me and beamed at his wife. "We have a beautiful daughter, and her timing is perfect; I am so glad I could see her before I had to leave for the office again."

This of course begs the question, wouldn't he have stayed there if I was born ten minutes later? I can't believe army discipline was that severe, but my dad's ideas were. He had to be back in the office by two, and, by golly, he was going to be back by two no matter what.

Three months later, my mother was in the park, pushing the pram with me in it, when she met her midwife. This lady, of course, immediately wanted to take a good look at "her" baby. Then her face fell and she said, "What on earth have you done to this child? She is starving thin."

My mother started to cry and said she did not know what to do. The midwife sent her at once to a clinic where my mother's milk was tested. It was completely inadequate, and she was told to feed me a bottle every three hours. In no time at all I was again a bouncing baby girl, and the midwife was content.

CHAPTER THREE

How my dad becomes champion in pistol shooting and I go naked.

My dad in his new uniform.

My German mom now had to learn to speak Dutch and learn to communicate with the servants; they only spoke Malayan. It can't have been easy for her, but she did it. We lived in a beautiful house in Tjimahi , but when I was three, we moved to Bandung. At that time, it was a lively country town, but today it is the Paris of Java. Hard to believe. We lived across from the military barracks where my father worked. He was now an under-lieutenant and very proud of it.

He became very proficient with firearms and was soon champion of the hand pistols. He was well-liked by his colleagues, and friends visited our place regularly. One night, my parents were having a good time with some of those friends when the door of the sitting room opened and I stood there, stark naked, covered in powder, cremes, and all kinds of other paraphernalia I had found on my mother's toiletry table. I spread my arms wide and said triumphantly, "It's all gone!" I was three years old at the time, which made my going naked not quite as shocking, but I certainly shocked the grown-ups at this moment. This event became one of my parents' favorite stories to tell, but at the time my mother was less than amused.

Another time, during siesta hour, I emptied my closet and pulled apart my entire bed by pulling out the mattress and the rest of the bedding. Then I deposited everything in the middle of the room. I now proceeded to pull all my clothing out of the closet and triumphantly built up my big heap. When I could not find anything more to improve the size of my "mountain" I went 'potty' and deposited that on top. I was nothing if not imaginative.

Edie at 3 years old.

For me, those years were warm and happy ones. All too soon they would be over. Europe was engulfed in war, and in May 1940 Rotterdam was bombed by the Germans without a declaration of war. My father advised my mother not to speak any German but to stick to Dutch. She was now a Dutch woman, he said, let it be so. She was twenty-four years old. Not only was she far from her own family but now she had to deny their very existence. Poor Mom.

CHAPTER FOUR

The Tempo Doeloe times are over and Holland goes to war.

The Dutch Netherlands Indies were primarily created during the nineteenth century, and the formerly independent indigenous states of the archipelago were brought under Dutch rule. The Netherlands Indies now became a political entity.

Before 1938 it had been a true paradise for the Dutch community, and those days were later aptly named the Tempo Doeloe (the good old times). The times when everything was the way it should be, according to the Dutch. Many would sigh later and remember with fondness how easy life had been back then. But in 1940 the rumblings of war in Europe and Hitler's rise to power were the topics of the day. The Dutch felt safe for a while, because Europe was far away. What worried most people was the fate of their loved ones in the old country. Could they stay out of the war? Could they stay neutral? The ties of Holland with their German neighbor had been strong over the years, but in Indonesia people waited with bated breath.

Then came that disastrous day in May 1940 when the news spread that Rotterdam had been bombed without there having been a declaration of war. Holland gave a token battle but was no match for mighty Germany, and they had to surrender.

Queen Wilhelmina left for London and stayed there during the entire war, but she sent her daughter, Princess Juliana, and her German husband, Prince Bernhard, to Canada. Princess Juliana stayed with her two children in Canada for the duration of the war, but our German Prince Bernard joined Queen Wilhelmina in London. Hard as it must have been for him, he considered himself now an integral part of the Dutch Royal family, and he did everything he could to help the allied forces.

Sometime during the war, he managed to visit Canada and his family. To everyone's delight, another princess was born nine months later. Her name was Margriet (Marguerite), and today she is one of the most beloved and admired members of the royal house of Holland, but her ties to her country of birth, Canada, have remained strong.

CHAPTER FIVE

*This is about wars, bomb shelters,
and how the enemy took over my school.*

Of all these things I knew not much, of course, except that people always seemed to be talking about "the old country" and "Hitler's war mongering." The mood was not good, and that did have an influence on how the overall atmosphere felt to a small child. Then the talk shifted to, "The Japanese," whoever they were, and that they had made a pact with Hitler. This seemed to be a very bad thing for us in Indonesia. People brought sandbags in and made one of the so-called gudangs (storage rooms) into a bomb shelter. We did too, of course. Then there were the alarm sirens that would go off during the day and also during the night, when we all had to run into the bomb-shelter; the servants with us, of course.

There were a number of huge bomb shelters built on the square in front of the military barracks where my dad had his office, and we kids loved to play in them. We could not know how we would long for those days of innocent and happy play, because not long afterwards something shocking happened. The Japanese attacked Pearl Harbor (December 8, 1941), with disastrous result for the Americans. This historic event is well documented today. Hitler was not pleased by this event as this meant that the Americans would now enter the war as well. The Germans would have liked to keep them out of the war.

The attack on Pearl Harbor was soon followed by the Japanese invasion of the Malay peninsula. It was rumored that this was the first step in a drive to take Indonesia's oil fields after the United States imposed an oil embargo on Japan. After the surprise victory over the U.S. at Pearl Harbour, the Japanese were unstoppable for a while.

"They took Guam and the Wake Islands around the time of the Pearl Harbor attack and invaded the Philippines, Burma, the Dutch East Indies, the Malay peninsula and after a few months captured Manila, Rangoon, Singapore, and Jakarta, the capital of Indonesia. The bold offensive gave Japan control over twenty million square miles of territory in Asia and the Pacific, five times the amount of territory controlled by Nazi Germany at the height of its power.[1]

The Japanese were no longer "just one of those Eastern nations," but a superpower, feared by everyone.

My first actual realization of war came in early 1942 when my babu (nanny) took me to school. When we got there, all the kids and parents and babus were milling around, not knowing what to do. The doors were closed, and one of my classmates said importantly, "The enemy has taken our school!"

That was the end of my schooling experience for the duration of the war. It had really reached us.

---

[1] Source: David Powers, BBC, February 17, 2011

CHAPTER SIX

The war, and how it happened.

Henry Hayes (2008) writes:

"In a brilliant move the Japanese attacked Pearl Harbor. Today, the whole world knows what happened; how many American ships had been destroyed in the aerial attack. And how the airport was bombed and almost destroyed every single plane, immobilizing the American force at the base. After the bombing of Pearl Harbor, the Dutch declared war on Japan.

(When I wrote this, I had to laugh. Yes, I bet Japan was really scared now! The fact was, of course, that the Dutch had to—as allies of the United States.)

The Japanese Imperial Army invaded the Dutch East Indies on January 1, 1942 under the pretext of creating the Greater East Asia Co-prosperity Sphere. During the last week of February 1942, the Japanese defeated American, British, and Dutch forces in the Battle of the Java Sea. The victory allowed Japan to break the Allied defensive perimeter (the Malay Barrier) and drive the Allied naval forces out of Southeast Asia, extending Japanese control to what is now Indonesia.

For the most part, the Japanese took Indonesia from the Dutch colonialists without a fight. The Dutch didn't have a large military force in the Dutch East Indies as Holland was occupied by the

Germans by that time. The Dutch navy in Indonesia was virtually destroyed. The Dutch colonial government abandoned Batavia (Jakarta) and surrendered it to Japanese forces in March 1942. Japanese soldiers marched into Batavia carrying the Indonesian "Red and White" flag along with the Japanese flag. Members of the Royal Dutch East Indies Army that remained were taken prisoner and transported to Singapore. About 65,000 Dutch and Indonesian soldiers were sent to labour camps. Some ended up working on the Burma Railroad in Thailand. Others worked in mines in Japan.

To add a personal note in this war recital, there was a kind of cynical little ditty going around at the time. It went like this:

Road, wit, blauw,
We komen gauw!
Witte vlag met de rode bal,
Wij zijn er al!

Meaning: Red, white, and blue (colors of the Dutch flag), We will soon be there!

White flag with red ball, We are there already!

The Japanese national flag is the white flag with the red ball, and they of course had already conquered the Netherlands East Indies, destroying our poor navy in the process. Not nice.

And that is when the war became a very personal thing to us all in Indonesia.

CHAPTER SEVEN

In which I do my first Holy Communion and discover that I am a very bad girl.

"The Burma Railway was a 415-kilometre (258-mile) railway between Ban Pong, Thailand, and Thanbyuzayat, Burma, built by the Empire of Japan in 1943 to support its forces in the Burma campaign of World War II. This railway completed the rail link between Bangkok, Thailand and Rangoon, Burma (now Yangon). The line was closed in 1947, but the section between NongPlaDuk and Nam Tok was reopened ten years later in 1957".

"Between 180,000 and 250,000 Southeast Asian civilian laborers (rōmusha) and about 61,000 Allied prisoners of war were subjected to forced labor during its construction. About 90,000 civilian laborers and about 16,000 Allied prisoners died."[2]

Soon after the Japanese invasion, my father was taken captive and forced to work on the railroad. My mother and I managed to stay out of the Bandung Camps for Women and Children for a while. We had been joined by a friend of my mother. Her name was Suzy Cools. She was a Belgian and she was young, beautiful, and very enterprising. She also had lots

---

2   From Wikipedia

of friends; they were the ones who gave us temporary housing when we needed it—in garages, gudangs, villas, whatever was available. We had discovered that we had to give our address to the Japanese every month, so after we gave our address we would move to another place. That is how we stayed out of the camps for a while. But it couldn't last.

I had made friends with a little girl of my own age. She and her mom were very nice to me. They went to church every Sunday, and I loved to go with them. One day, my little friend said that she was going to have her first holy Communion. Was I also going to have it? We could do it together. I loved the idea, especially as we were to have beautiful new white dresses for this occasion. My mom was happy for me that I had made friends with another girl, but she did not inquire too much about what was going on while I was with that girl and her mom. She had other pressing things on her mind, like, *Is it time to move again? And, where do we go this time? And how are we going to pay for it?!*

Suzy Cools at 17.

Now I get that, but at the time I certainly did not understand her attitude.

I had told her that I needed a white dress for church, but she nixed the idea. "You don't need another dress. There are far more important things to consider than a new dress."

I went to my girlfriend's mom and told her what my mom had said. She looked sad for a moment, but then her face cleared up and she said, "Never mind. I will make you a new white dress!" I was ecstatic, of course. I was told to do many "Hail Marys" by the nuns and I obediently knelt down and said them faithfully. I did not really know who Mary and Jesus and God were, but I loved everything I had to do. I loved the whole atmosphere in the church. It was beautiful and very quiet, and I felt that it was such a serene and happy place to be.

Finally, the big day was there. I had taken my new white dress home and put in on happily in anticipation of a wonderful and exciting day. With a beaming face I showed my mom how lovely I looked, but she got very angry. "I don't need other people to make clothes for my child! I shall dress you as I see fit." She took off my new white dress and told me to put on a little white skirt with a dark red top.

I cried and cried and said that I had to wear white; everyone was going to be in white. "Please, please, let me wear my white dress."

She refused, and threatened to keep me home, instead of letting me go to church.

I subdued my tears and left to tell my tale of woe to my girlfriend and her mom. Her mom was distressed. She had not known it would cause such trouble for me. She calmed me down and said, "Well, we'll just go as we are. Jesus loves you no matter what you wear." I was consoled again. At least I could still go to my beloved church.

We duly walked down the aisle, with me trying to hide my red top. I did everything I was told to do and was happy. Afterwards, my girlfriend's mom prepared a festive lunch and we had a great time.

A few days later, my mom met someone while out shopping for groceries. This lady congratulated her on her daughter's first holy Communion. My mother stared at her and said, "But we are not Catholic; we are Protestant."

The other lady turned all red and said, "But that is terrible. That is not allowed at all. It is a disgrace that you let your daughter do this."

I don't remember my mom reprimanding me or even talking to me about it. She probably shrugged it off, as there were so many more important things to think about and do.

The next Sunday I went again with my friends to church. When we got there, I was stopped by a nun. She was very severe and shook her finger at me. "You did something very bad! You are not Catholic; you should not have done a holy Communion. And," she continued, "we never want to see you here in our church again. Do you understand?"

I was so shocked at what I heard that I could not say a word. My girlfriend's mom heard all this and shook her head in disbelief. "Why did you not tell us that you are not Catholic?" she said.

"I did not know I was not Catholic; I don't know what that means," I sniffled. I did not know I had to be Catholic to go to their church.

The nun had scared me so much that I was a very subdued little seven-year-old who came home that Sunday. I now realized that praying was bad if you were not Catholic (whatever that meant). And that Hail Marys also should not be said. From that day on I was terrified of nuns and anything to do with a church.

CHAPTER EIGHT

*In which the uncles become aunties
and the Japs pay us a visit.*

By the time September 1942 rolled around, we had moved into a beautiful villa somewhere in the cooler regions of Bandung. We loved it there, but we knew that we only had one month to stay there. The house had a lovely verandah behind the house with great built-in flower beds around the deck. These flowers hid a secret; the containers could be lifted up and underneath the owner had created a perfect hiding place for several people.

Auntie Suzy (as I now called her) had several friends who were trying to leave Java and go to England to fight in the war, but this was very difficult. They were in hiding all the time, trying to find connections to help them escape. Suzie had proposed to them to stay for a few weeks at our house; the hiding place was there in case the Japs decided to visit us. I was taught to call them all 'Auntie'. It was hard for a seven-year-old to remember to do that, but we practiced a lot.

In the villa every day passed without any sign of the Japs, but I was not allowed to go beyond the yard of the house, which had a large wall all around it. One day, however, as much as we had been fearing and expecting it, it was still a shock—the knock on the front door sounded loud and authoritative.

We knew at once what it was, but for an instant we all froze. Then the "uncles" jumped up and began removing the flower beds. They hastily slid into their hiding place and my mom and Auntie Suzy quickly put the flowers back in place. Then Auntie Suzy ran to the front door and opened it. There were two Japanese officers, who bowed politely. Auntie Suzy, equally polite, bowed deeply to them, and then invited them in.

I do not know what excuse they gave for their visit, but now I think they had their eyes on the house for their own purpose. They checked out the entire house, and went to the outbuildings, opening every single room on the way. It was very scary. My mom kept me close to her, admonishing me every time I wanted to speak. "Shhht. I will tell you everything later, but not now!"

The officers finally left, satisfied I guess, that we were not harbouring any forbidden persons.

The "aunties" did not make a move for at least ten minutes. I guess they were afraid the Japanese officers would come back and surprise them. Finally, Auntie Suzy and my mom lifted the flower beds up and told them it was safe to come out again. It had been a harrowing experience for all of us. I can understand now that my mother must have been terrified at me opening my mouth. I could have innocently said all the wrong things. After all, I was only a little girl.

I was very conscious that the small men with yellow complexions, riding their bicycles around town were dangerous to us. They were "The Enemy." I was taught to bow to them when we passed them in town on our grocery shopping trips. But I also heard the derogatory comments from the white people about having to bow to the Japs. Everybody found it a crazy law the Japs had passed. The Dutch figured they had to bow because the Japs had conquered us. It was their way of showing that they were now superior to us.

Bowing to the Japs.
Picture by Ann Cooper

It was only much later that I realized the possible truth of the matter. The Japanese people have a habit of bowing to each other. It is merely a question of politeness and a way of honoring their elders and betters. It is just possible that they were simply trying to teach us their ways. I don't think it would have done any good explaining this to the white population at the time. The Japs were The Enemy and an enemy can never do anything that is good in the eyes of the conquered people.

Of whom I was one, little as I was. And I have to admit that it took me a long, long time to get over the feeling of revulsion and fear whenever I saw a Japanese face. I am half-German, but that did not prevent me from fearing and disliking German people. I had been indoctrinated for years with stories of how bad the Japs were and how bad the Germans and Hitler were.

CHAPTER NINE

In which we have to admit defeat and enter our first camp.

One day, Auntie Suzy and I ventured out into town to buy groceries and other necessities. Suddenly there was a lot of noise and shouting around us, and we, and others like us, were herded together and then taken into the Kempeitai for interrogation. *(The Military Police Corps served as the military police of the Japanese Army from 1881 —1945. It draws parallels with Nazi Germany's Gestapo, in that it was a secret police force rather than an overt operation. They committed many atrocities over the years.)*

Belgium, by now, was also at war with Germany, so Suzy (who was a Belgian) had to go into a camp. Later, my mother (being German) was offered the choice; stay outside the camp or go with Suzy wherever they would send her. She had no choice—we had no money, and no matter how little, we did need food to survive. My mother decided she and I would go with Suzy into the camp.

Auntie Suzy had a small pet, a little dachshund she was very fond of. Little Winnie had just given birth to ten puppies and we could not leave her behind, of course. So, one day my mother and Auntie Suzy loaded up a cart, drawn by a skinny karbouw (tropical buffalo). Everything we were allowed to take was on it, and on top sat I with little Winnie and her ten babies on my lap.

And so we entered the gates of Tjihapit Camp. Tjihapit was the biggest of the Bandung Camps for Women and Children in Southeast Asia. It began as a suburb in northeast Bandung, from where all non-Europeans were evicted at short notice, in order to create the camp. With time, the density of home occupancy grew to thirty persons per single-family dwelling. If we had known what awaited us, my mother would have thought ten times about accepting to go into any camp, money or not. I can still remember passing the guards at the gate as we entered the camp. It did not seem so bad at that moment. There were just houses and streets and people milling around. Ha!

We were taken to a very nice house and were already congratulating ourselves that we could live there. Then we were led around the main house towards the long line of gudangs; we did not understand what we had to do there. A harsh-sounding Dutch lady pointed to a narrow kitchen, which was not used as such, and said, "Here are your quarters now." We stood there and stared with round eyes at the old kitchen of the house. There was a counter and it had a tap for water; that was good. That was also all there was…Auntie Suzy and my mom went and managed to unload the stuff off the wagon and bring it in. They squeezed their mattresses into a corner and mine went on the countertop. Most of our stuff was put along the corridor that ran past the gudangs.

KISMET

Several times a day, everyone had to line up to get food. We carried stacked tin pans for that purpose. We all had to line up in person unless we were too sick. I remember always being pleased to line up, as this meant FOOD. It wasn't great but at least it was something to eat…

My mom was prone to getting malaria attacks and was often not able to accompany us. Auntie Suzy was always ready for some fun and as we were in the long, long line-up waiting to be given our food, she introduced rope jumping. I remember how much we all enjoyed doing the rope jumping with her, while our tin cans stayed in the line-up. We used to laugh and try to better each other all the time. This way the waiting in the line-up was not too difficult.

But then, one day I got a toothache. There were doctors and dentists in the camp, of course, but they did not have any type of medication…So, there I sat, waiting to have my tooth pulled. I know it must have just been a baby-tooth but it still was not easy to pull it. And to do it without any painkillers? The doctor said afterwards that she was glad she had developed nerves of steel because my screams were loud enough to alert the guards at the entrance gate! I survived, but dentists have never been my favourite people. I know, most people don't like to go to the dentist, but my dislike was perhaps a little bit more pronounced than most.

There was a lady in our house who had three sons. The oldest was fourteen, number two was eleven, and the youngest was eight. The greatest fear for mothers of boys was that their sons would be taken away. The age at which boys were transferred to men's camps dropped from fifteen at the start of the war, to thirteen then eleven, until by 1944 boys of ten were being transported. As they waited to climb on to the lorries they would cling to their mothers, not knowing whether they'd ever see them again. I could not understand why they had to go away until I was much older. Poor kids. I was a girl. I did not have to leave my mother; that much was clear to me and it made me very happy.

Then one day Auntie Cobie got the news; her oldest boy, who was now fifteen had to be sent away. It was a very sad day, and everyone was grumbling about the Japs and trying to console Auntie Cobie, saying that the war would surely be over very soon. She was terrified that her next boy would be sent away as well, but as he was only twelve she thought she had time. Unfortunately, the Japs changed the rules. Now boys of twelve were being sent away. And that's how it went. Auntie Cobie had to send her second boy away too. Auntie Cobie cried so hard that I could not forget this event for the longest time. Her youngest son of ten was sleeping under their klamboe (mosquito netting) and I was in ours but we were next to each other. We became the best of friends, whispering to each other at night about everything. A while after the war, when we were briefly in Holland, we found Auntie Cobie's address and went to see her. All three boys had survived, and the reunion was a very happy one.

CHAPTER TEN

In which we cry a lot and are moved to another camp.

Not long after this event, we got the news that we were being transported to another camp "somewhere in the jungle." We were allowed to take with us the barest minimum. Not wanting to leave anything behind that the Japs could use, the women had started huge bonfires. Here everything we could not take was burned. I had a few beautiful books of fairy tales that we could not take with us. These too were put into the fire. Even today when I remember watching those books burn, I still get tears in my eyes. It was so hard to see that. I just could not understand why all those marvelous things had to be burned. Couldn't they be saved for later? Then I would be roughly told to shut up. "We don't want the enemy to get any of our things," was the answer.

The Japs now confiscated all personal effects like passports and birth certificates. We could only take with us a total of 20 kg (44 lbs). This included all household items such as chamber pots, dishes, books, clothing, bedding, etc. It was so hard to choose what to keep and what to leave behind, even for a child such as I was.

Then it was time. We were leaving. We walked to the train station, carrying our luggage, and then everyone was herded into long wagons with benches on either side and one bench in the middle. We got to sit on that middle bench; nothing to lean against. The wooden shutters were closed and after hours and hours of waiting we finally left. It was hot, there were no toilets, and we were not given any water for a very long time. Children were crying, mothers were crying, the Japanese were yelling at us, and I just tried to find a place to sit or lie in that was not too uncomfortable.

I so remember that train ride. First of all, there was the waiting to leave the station. The wooden shutters had been closed early on, which prevented any fresh air from getting into the wagons. We had some water with us but that disappeared very quickly as the heat became more and more difficult to take. Finally, finally, the train started to move and everybody perked up. Now we would soon know where we were going. Maybe it was going to be a much better place than we had before.

One hour went by. Another hour went by—no change. We were not allowed to open the shutters, so the heat (and the smells) got worse and worse. As there were no toilets, we had to pee in the pee pots we had taken with us. The women started to chant that they wanted water and fresh air, but the Japanese guards shushed them harshly. Now it is clear why the shutters could not be opened; they did not want the local population to know that a transport of women and children was in progress.

The train ride lasted two days. Once we stopped, we were given water and could empty pee pots and even clean ourselves up a bit under a tap. I don't think we got any food. At any rate, I can't remember eating anything, and we never left the platform next to the train. Too soon we were told to get back inside and the second half of that hellish trip began. On the middle bench, we were all trying to lean against each other; you can sit straight up only so long. I had found myself a little hollow on the bags lying in the path between the benches. I did sleep but woke up frequently. It was a trip from hell and back. All the kids kept asking their moms, "How long will this last, Mom?

"Don't know, don't know..." was the mumbled answer, so finally we stopped asking.

At long last, the train started to slow down and we dared to hope that we had reached our destination. Then we passed a sign that said "Ambarawa Station." We finally knew, or thought we knew, where we were being sent. We climbed out of the train with our little luggage and then had to wait until everyone was out. We wondered where our camp was but could see nothing. Ambarawa was not our destination but the little town of Banju Biru, five kilometres south of Ambarawa. We looked for trucks to take us there but then were told to start walking. And so we walked and walked, again carrying our own luggage. It was good to stretch our legs, but soon the little ones started to cry and had to be picked up. We were so relieved when we finally reached the entrance to our new prison.

"Banyu Biru," translated from Indonesian, means "Blue Waters." The name may have been poetic, but this was no lake—it was a swamp; a breeding ground of the dreaded malaria mosquito. The compound—known as "BanjuBiru X" for the duration of the war—was formerly an army barracks (then abandoned) and before that a prison. It had high walls, buildings with barred windows, the sewage ran straight from the toilets to open gutters, and the smell was described as putrid. On arrival, we were queued for several hours to be processed and registered and were then billeted."[3]

We were placed in the second big hall on the left side with a hundred other women and children. There was one toilet at the end of the hall, which could be used during the night or when you were too sick to move and had to be brought there.

I can still see myself as we came to the hall in which we were to be placed. We had a stretch of 135 cm of bed space on the raised platform, (which ran from one end of the hall to the other) for my mom, Auntie Suzy, and myself; 45 cm per person. I got that this was where we were going to sleep; under a klamboe (mosquito netting) for three. Cozy. But then I looked around and said, "Mom, I understand that we are going to sleep here, but where are we going to live?" I was still used to four walls around our living area. This was not it. This hall was enormous, or so it seemed to an eight-year old.

My mom sadly shook her head and said, "Right where we sleep, darling."

---

[3] From a Quote from Henriette Thomas (nee Kuneman).

This proved to be our daily menu:

Tea early in the morning before roll call
(no sugar, no milk, of course).
Breakfast: a bowl of starch (literally).
Lunch: a cup of boiled rice, a heaped tablespoon
of boiled green cabbage and a heaped teaspoon of
sambal, a sort of Spanish pepper.
Tea in the afternoon (see morning tea).
Dinner: starch soup with a few leaves of cabbage.
One could count
the small pieces.[4]

I was never able to eat the small bowl of breakfast starch. I tried and tried but it just would not go down—so icky it was. One day, my mom had one of her malaria attacks and was very sick. Auntie Suzy said to me that I had to eat the starch as my mom would worry so much if I did not eat it. "Do it for your mom, honey." So, I went outside with the bowl, sat down on the stoop, and ate the starch while the tears ran down my cheeks. Not five minutes later everything came out again. My stomach just could not digest that horrible stuff.

But the first night was the worst yet because of the horrible bed bugs we encountered. They seemed to come from everywhere and we had no way to stop this invasion of our bodies. Everyone was red and scratched the next morning. We

---

4 Memories of the Dutch East Indies: From Plantation Society to Prisoner of Japan by Elizabeth Van Kampen

were allowed to take out our bedding once a week and also the klamboes and what sheets we still had to let the sun do its work. That always helped a little. The problem was that this was hard work for bodies that had no resistance to anything, especially for my mom with her two or three times-a-month malaria attacks. She would so often succumb to another malaria attack after the weekly airing of our bedding. This was simply because our bodies were so weak any kind of extra work proved too much for many of the women.

CHAPTER ELEVEN

In which we learn to eat snails but have very little food.

Everyone who was able had to do some kind of work, of course. My mom always tried to work in the kitchen as it was sometimes possible for her to take an extra little bite home to us; yes, mostly to me, of course. Auntie Suzy developed beri-beri (water in the legs). This was very dangerous as it would go higher and higher and, in the end, come to the heart. That was it then.

Two women carrying heavy soup pot.
Picture by Ann Cooper.

The only remedy that was found by the doctors in the camp was SNAILS. There were lots of snails in the beginning of our camp time. The doctors said that they contained what was lacking in the diet of patients with beriberi. They gave each person with this sickness three snails a day. They were cooked and then consumed. Suzy always gave one of her snails to me. I think it was the snails that kept me alive during this time. I still like eating snails, but then in the form of escargots, prepared French-style with lots of garlic and butter!

Auntie Coby had her bed next to ours so her youngest son, my age, was my best friend. We would whisper with each other through our respective klamboes every night before going to sleep. It was a great help to have such a friend.

We slowly got used to living like this. There were no more hidden radios that could tell us the latest news, so we had to rely on any little bit the Japs themselves would let slip. Occasionally the women who had duty outside of the camps would meet up with others from another camp. If they had a chance, they would exchange their experiences and ask for any kind of news. It was never much.

We children had our tasks too. We had to pull the weeds around the buildings. An older girl (fifteen or sixteen) would supervise us. She would also try to teach us some little songs and, depending on which Japanese officer would come around to check up on us, they would let us sing. Some of the other officers would growl, "Work, no sing!" We were very afraid of them and would pull weeds as if our lives depended on it!

One of the supervising girls tried to teach us the alphabet by writing the letters in the dirt with a stick. This was an absolute no-no, so we had to be very careful not to be seen. No teaching of any kind was allowed. For me, though, it was very helpful. I had been taught some of the basics during my few months in school so I was very anxious to learn more.

A few months later somebody had a book on William Tell. Remember, the guy who shot the apple off his son's head? The book was completely loose by now, so the first person would read the first page, then pass it on to the next, and so on. I put myself in this line-up as well, even though I was not proficient enough yet. However, I would pass my page along when the others did and start on the next one with gusto. In no time at all I became a voracious reader, and today I still am.

CHAPTER TWELVE

*In which my mom gets skinnier and
Auntie Suzy gets bigger.*

My mom got skinnier and skinnier and Auntie Suzy got bigger and bigger with her beriberi. Her legs were terribly swollen, and snails were not always to be found anymore. I did not get too skinny as my thyroid glands did not work very well. The doctors were always pleased to see me as I was one of the few kids who was not just skin and bones. Unfortunately, this played havoc with my body during my teen years. I got quite heavy, could not run very well, and so never was chosen to be on any kind of team. This was sometimes hard to take, but there wasn't much I could do about it. "No, Edie, you can't have a chocolate." "No, Edie, don't take a second portion, you had enough." I was young and fit and hungry all the time. Food was important to me, after the horrible war years of not having anything.

Even though I looked healthier than most kids there, I was not immune to all the diseases that were going around. I developed jaundice, which gave me stomach aches and made me lose weight. Soon I was not that healthy-looking anymore. By the time Christmas approached, I had developed very nasty open ulcers on my legs and could not walk anymore. My mother had to carry me to the wash area and to the toilet in our hall. I felt very sorry for myself. I also got dysentery. No, it was not a very pleasant time.

My mother had developed an annoying habit of dreaming out loud about pastries. She would talk about Black Forest cakes "And put lots of whipped cream on it, please!" and all kinds of other delicacies we could only dream about, as she did! The other women got so annoyed they would get up and shake her awake to stop her from saying these things out loud. She told us later that she never got to taste any of those delicious cakes and pies of her dreams; she'd always wake up just as she was about to take a bite, poor thing!

Then it was Christmas 1944. We had nothing to celebrate with, of course. But our hall did get some women together and one woman told the story of Jesus; how he was born to save us and that he died for us on the cross. I whispered to my mom, "Was Jesus a Catholic, Mom?."

She said, "You prayed to God then, and God is the father of Jesus."

Oh, yes, I remembered how happy I had been to go to the Catholic church at first, but then how I was told off by the nun in no uncertain terms. I was very wary of this Jesus; he must be a Catholic too, and I was not a Catholic.

I had trouble taking all this in, but when they started to sing Christmas songs, I really liked it very much. They had gathered close to where I was lying with my bandaged legs, and I remember how peaceful and happy I felt at that moment.

CHAPTER THIRTEEN

In which I am shocked at the way the Japs punish someone and in which a large snake tries to eat a woman.

One day, when I was better again, I was walking with my mom close to where the Japanese over-seers had their offices. Suddenly, we saw that in front of the building a woman was kneeling on the dirt and gravel with a bamboo behind her knees. Every time she leaned back, she would put weight on the bamboo. This must have been very painful; bamboos are not always smooth. This seemed to be one of the punishments the Japs had for women who had done something wrong in their eyes. I was completely shocked when I saw that. I had become used to seeing women with bald heads, as this was another punishment the Japs had devised. But we saw this woman sit in the full sun without a hat, of course, and were told by somebody else that she had been sitting there for hours.

By now she was trembling and crying but the Japs did not let her go. Finally, she fainted, which must have been a relief for her. They told some of the women who were near to take her away. They quickly did and later the doctor said that she had severe sun-stroke, which was not surprising, plus a very sore body all over. She had been completely dehydrated and would take a while to recover.

Even the children soon learn to bow deeply.
Picture by Ann Cooper.

Even something like this, or to have their heads shaven, or being hit in the face did not deter the women from trying to get food from under the gedek (fence). They would exchange whatever they had to give for an egg or some vegetables. One day, Auntie Suzy managed to get a small piece of bacon. Oh, my, were we all excited. They managed to fry the bacon somehow in a far corner of the compound, and I still remember how incredibly good it tasted, mixed with the bit of rice which was our lunch. Even today, I absolutely adore bacon. But, alas, I still have a tendency to easily put on weight, so it doesn't happen often. But, sometimes, I indulge and, when I do, I still close my eyes and remember the wonder of tasting something so utterly delicious to taste buds that had been deprived for so long.

Our Japanese overlords were often very cruel, but they did have their uses sometimes. One day I went to the "loo"; this was a ditch in the ground, a distance away from our hall. Two planks were laid across the ditch for each loo. There was only a light bamboo separation between each so-called loo and no front door, but it gave us at least some privacy. We always took a bottle of water with us as we of course did not have toilet paper. I was just pulling up my pants when I heard the woman next to me scream so loud and so agonizingly that I rushed out to see why she was screaming. Then I screamed too because this huge snake was twisting itself rapidly around her body. Our combined screams had women run to us from everywhere, and even the Japanese guards came running. One of them had a gun and he started waving it around, trying to find a way to kill the snake. I did not see the end of the battle because some of the women took me away and tried to console me from the terrible thing I had seen.

Later I found out that the guard had succeeded in killing the snake; it probably was a python. He had saved the woman's life. But that could have been me if the snake had come from my side. It was unthinkable—to be killed like that! The trauma from that experience has lasted a lifetime. Even today I always want the toilet lid closed because "You never know what can come from down there!" No matter how many times I'm told that nothing can possibly come from "down there" I won't believe it. "Close the lid!" I shout. "Please close the lid!"

In the meantime, diseases were rampant, the bedbugs were biting harder than ever, the food was at the very minimum, and there was no way to use soap to fight head lice as we never had any soap. Yuck, I still shiver in disgust when I think of it!

We had a covered place where there was a well. I remember there only being one well, but I may be wrong. We called the place Algeria, but I never discovered why. Probably because it seemed so far away to go to wash oneself. That's how the laundry was done too, just with water. It was better than nothing, I guess, but not overly effective against the bugs.

CHAPTER FOURTEEN

In which the Japanese emperor admits defeat and we get to find food again.

Then, in August 1945, suddenly it seemed as if the Japs were not so officious anymore. They hardly ever came to check up on us and they were lax in watching for the exchange of goods under the barbed wire, which encouraged the women, of course, to be more and more blatant in their efforts to get some food exchanged. What could it mean? Why were they so negligent? Did they know something we didn't?

I had my tenth birthday on the 21st of August and was quite excited about it. My mother had managed to exchange something with another woman for an old, knitted, red cotton top. She had pulled it apart and knitted me a new top. I was so pleased. What an exciting birthday present!

In the meantime, the Japs became more and more forgiving around us, and acted as if they didn't really care anymore what we did. Finally, we found out why. On the 24th of August, there was another roll call, and we all trouped outside as usual. The officers came and stood in front of us. After the usual procedure of standing at attention, then bowing, and finally standing straight again, the officer in charge said, "The Japanese emperor has seen fit to end the war. You are free to go." There was complete silence for a moment. Everyone seemed too stunned to react, but then cheers went up and everybody was hugging everybody else and laughing and crying at the same time.

The Japanese emperor, Hirohito, had indeed seen fit to end the war as the Japanese Supreme Council had realized that there was no way to win it anymore. The Allied Forces had demanded from Japan an unconditional surrender on July 26, 1945, and if they did not surrender The Allied Forces had threatened a complete and utter destruction of the country. It took the atomic bombings of Hiroshima and then Nagasaki (August 6th and August 9th respectively), as well as the entrance into the battle by Russia on the side of the angels, before the decision to surrender was finally made by the Japanese High Council.

All these details we only found out afterwards, of course. The first thing we did after hearing the exciting news was to leave the camp to try and find food. We took whatever little things we had left to use in exchange for the food and started walking. I remember the three of us; Auntie Suzy, my mom, and I walked and walked until we found a place that sold food. We asked for their menu and ate the first course, the second, until the last course. Then we started all over again. Then we went back to the camp—where else could we go?

When we'd left the camp, we had met many skinny men coming towards our camp. This was very exciting. They were the prisoners of war who had been placed in a neighboring camp, and who now were trying to find their families. We did not recognize anyone. On the way back to the camp I was overcome by too much food and my weakened immune system. I had to lie down on the ground because I was fainting. My mom and Auntie Suzy were worried and did not know what to do. They hunkered down beside me, trying to make me feel better. Then, suddenly, there was a voice beside us that said, "What is wrong with the girl?" It was a young man. When he heard what had happened and where we wanted to go, he offered to carry me all the way to the camp. We were so grateful, especially myself. It felt so safe to be carried by a man, even though he was just as skinny as the rest of us were.

Unfortunately, I was not the only one whose stomach had not been able to handle the influx of real food so suddenly, after years of starving. That night many women and children died. It was sad and so ironic that it was eating decent food that killed them in the end!

The next day we went again to the same place to eat. We were a bit more restrained this time, after what we had seen during the night—so many people dying after eating much more than they had had in years.

There had been lots of excitement during the day as the Red Cross had sent all kinds of extra foods and messages from husbands, sons, and fathers. We had not heard anything about my dad's whereabouts and my mom was very worried. Finally, there came long lists of men who had died—my dad was on that list.

My mom collapsed and Auntie Suzy had her hands full with her. Then she checked the list again and said, "Hetty, it may not be your Johnny who died. Keep your hopes up; this may be a different

Smidt." Yes, that was our family name. There were several Smidts in the list, but it gave my mom hope that Suzy could be right. The next day we received a missive from my dad. He was alive and he was in Bangkok. We were jubilant, of course. I felt so happy that I still had a father, although I did not remember him very well.

CHAPTER FIFTEEN

In which the rebels are rumoured to bomb our camp.

During the day, shots had been fired from the trees surrounding the camps. We were told that many of the Malayan people had revolted against the Dutch; they now wanted to have their independence. We had to be very careful where we walked and could not go near the windows. The next day, the British sent over a group of Ghurkas. The Ghurkas had been part of the British Army for almost 200 years, and were fearsome Nepalese fighters. Their motto was, "Better to die than to be a coward." We were so lucky to get them there; they saved our lives.

They installed themselves by the windows and proceeded to shoot down anyone climbing the trees outside. We were told to take our mattresses and sleep under the platform on which we normally slept. This was really scary. Rats scrambled around, cockroaches climbed over us, and the bedbugs followed us faithfully. A lot of crying and whining was going on at night. The Ghurkas took turns staying by the windows as the shots from outside kept coming. We became very fond of the brave Ghurkas. Some of them got hit by the bullets themselves.

Then we heard a rumour that our camp was going to be bombed the next day by the rebels. They were told by Sukarno, who later became the first president of an independent

Indonesia, to "Kill the white dogs!" We were told that that night we would all be transported to somewhere else, if they could possibly get it done, in order to save our lives.

Late at night, trucks arrived and we were loaded up. We kids had chamber pots on our heads to protect us from any possible bullets. It was a very scary night.

The next day our camp was indeed bombed thoroughly. We barely escaped with our lives, though nothing much else. After driving for many hours, we came to a place that apparently just had been freed from the rebels; they had to take us somewhere—it was hard to find any place for us to go to. The rebels really had the whole country in a battle mode. Here again we had to be very careful not to expose ourselves to any snipers.

One morning—we only stayed for a short week—I was standing at the top of some stairs outside of the main building on my way down, when I heard the snipers again. I quickly ran down as fast as I could, but the Ghurka who had been just behind me was not so lucky. He was shot and his body rolled down the stairs next to me, blood going everywhere. I cried bitterly and ran around, trying to find my mom and Aunt Suzy.

Finally, I found them and tried to tell them what had just happened. "Mommy, they were shooting again and then this Ghurka fell down the stairs and there was blood everywhere. Oh, Mommy, I am so scared. I want to leave from here. Please, please, let's leave from here!"

It took a long time to calm me down.

The whole situation in this place became untenable. The rebels became more and more aggressive and there were not enough Ghurkas to successfully defend us. At last there were the trucks again late at night, and we were all hastily shoved into them and taken away, one truck after another, as silently as possible.

At last, after a very long drive, we came to a town on the north shore of Java called Semarang. There we were placed in a reasonably pleasant house with many of the others, but we were pleased to stay put for a while. We still had to be careful about going outside, but we did manage to go for walks and we did get to eat good food again. The Red Cross people were wonderful; they helped us with everything.

Aunt Suzy, in the meantime, had been taken away while we were still in the camp in Banyu-Biru. She and other sick women were taken to a hospital somewhere—I am not sure where, because of her beriberi. It had become so bad that she found it harder and harder to walk, and she needed to be treated as quickly as possible.

My mom and I lived in Semarang for several months, waiting for news from my dad. He wanted us to come to Bangkok to join him there, but it was hard to find the necessary means to transport us there. We kept hoping that we would see him before Christmas, and every day we looked out for news from him. Once in a while, some of the other women got news from their husbands, and then they would leave us with big smiles on their faces.

My mom was always happy for them but also very jealous—why couldn't we get the news that we could go and join my dad in Bangkok? Then we heard; there was a ship going to Bangkok and we were going to be on it. What excitement, what happiness, and what nerves it took (my mom's) to get ready to board the ship. I had one pair of shoes and so had my mom. We both had something to wear, though it wasn't pretty after years in a concentration camp. But there we finally went.

A group of other women and children were going as well. There was quite a large number of us that were going to Bangkok. We were brought to a quay in the harbour of Semarang and had to step onto a large barge.

I was very excited to see the sea for the first time, but the huge expanse of water was very intimidating and I started to feel frightened. I grabbed my mom's hand and stayed close to her. "Is it safe, Mom? Are we not going to fall into the water?"

My mom reassured me that all would be well. Then we left.

I thought we would go to Bangkok on this barge, but they laughed when I said that. "No, we are going to go on a very big ship and it will take us a week to get there." Then they pointed into the distance and there I saw a small round object like a barrel sitting in the water.

I was horrified! How were we all going to fit into that little barrel? I felt the blood drain from my face and I clung onto my mom's hand. She kept saying it would be all right, and don't worry. "We will all fit easily, you will see when we come nearer."

As we drew nearer and nearer, the barrel became bigger and bigger, and so did my eyes.

The explanation was easy, of course. I had spent years in camps and knew nothing about distance. My world had been what I saw around me and nothing was really far away. I had had very little or no schooling in all those years. Or ever. I had been too young. Now, I was getting a very big lesson about how objects could seem small from afar, while getting bigger as one got closer. But the biggest lesson on that journey to Bangkok was yet to come.

CHAPTER SIXTEEN

Where I know that the end of life is near but no-one else does.

There were hang mats somewhere down in the lower regions of the boat, and that was where we were going to sleep. Everything was a complete surprise to me, especially that vast expanse of water. I don't remember much about the eating facilities, or whether anything was organized to keep us children a bit entertained—I remember nothing but the water. I stood at the railing as often as I could and just stared. I was convinced that we would fall off the earth at a certain line in the water.

I looked at all the other people, saw them laughing, joking, happy at all the things that now were possible again, and I thought, "Poor guys; they don't know that we are all going to fall off the earth in a very short time." I thought I was the only one who realized this. Every night again I was surprised that we had not done so yet, but I was happy. One more day to be here. One more day of living this life. Then it would be all over. My heart was dark with foreboding. I wanted to ask my mother about this, but she was so happy to be going to my father in Bangkok that I did not want to take away her happiness. So, I continued to suffer by myself.

The travel to Bangkok took a week, but it seemed to me to be much longer. Every night again it was a relief that nothing had happened yet, but the next day I was at the railing again to stare at that dark line in the distance. There, there it would happen!

On the seventh day there suddenly was no more black line in the distance. There was land in sight instead. I did not understand how that was possible, but it really was so. My relief was almost tragic. We had survived this travel and were still on our earth. How wonderful, and what a miracle that this had happened.

CHAPTER SEVENTEEN

Disembarkation time!

We children were of course in the front. We all were in a rush to get to firm ground again. And we were also excited because somewhere among all those people waiting on the cargo quay, we could maybe find our daddies!

I was wearing some kind of dress and some very old sandals that had belonged to various other kids. I did not care about that. I turned around to check that my mother was in sight. She had her hands full with the last of our things. She too wore an old dress, which did not do much for her, but at least she was dressed as nicely as she could be. And she wore some kind of shoes. Poor Mom. She was in for quite a shock that very same night.

I saw a military man with short-cropped red hair waving us on. "This way, ladies, a little faster please. Come on, can you hurry it up a little? A lot of people will still have to disembark." I ignored him, of course, and meandered along, looking around me with great interest. There were many Malayans and that scared me a little after all we had gone through to get to safety, but these ones seemed friendly. Then I heard a cry behind me "Johnny! Johnny!"

I turned around and saw that the red-headed military man had his arms around my mom and they were both crying and laughing at the same time. Could that really be my dad? I did not remember him very well. I approached slowly and suddenly my mom saw me. She turned to the man and said, "Johnny, this is your daughter, Edie."

He looked at me, picked me up in his arms and hugged me so tight I thought I was going to get crushed. "My daughter and my wife, after all those years! I can't believe it!" and he started to cry again. Now all three of us were crying, but those were happy tears. All around us the same thing was happening. What a happy day this was. I had a real father again, not just a mother and lots of aunties.

My father signaled to somebody to take over his job and took my mom and me in a jeep to his camp. They had arranged as many places as possible for couples and their children to live there temporarily. My dad had managed to arrange a garage for us with two beds and some chairs in it. To us it sounded fine; we were not exactly spoiled. Then my dad said that he would take my mom out that night "on the town." She was so excited. Her eyes sparkled at the idea.

The rest of the day was a bit chaotic, of course, but finally it was time for me to go to sleep. My mom had washed her one "good" dress and ironed it, and she had washed her hair and styled it as well as she could. She only had the shoes she had arrived, in so she cleaned those and then showed herself to me. "How do I look, Edie?"

"You look wonderful, Mom," I said. And I meant it. After the years in the camps she had not had much chance to use real soap or to wash her hair with real shampoo. And off they went.

After a while I fell asleep, although it was hard at first. Everything was so strange and the noises were so different, and I was not used to being alone.

The next morning, I opened my eyes to see my mother was up and dressed already. I asked her how she had enjoyed her outing. She half-smiled and said that it had been fine, but I knew something was not right. Later, she told me what had happened. Here is the story in her own words:

"I was so pleased to go out with your father again. It was such a wonderful, wonderful experience to be near him again. And I felt really almost glamorous, with nicely washed hair and a clean dress. Then we came to the night club where we were also going to have our dinner. I did not have eyes enough to look around me. It seemed as if there had been no war here. Everything was lit up, and everyone was dressed in the finest and most beautiful outfits possible.

"There was plenty of great food and the music was wonderful. I should have been thrilled but I felt myself shrink with each new woman I beheld. They were all so sophisticated. They smoked cigarettes from a long pipe, were all heavily made up, their hair had been done by professionals, and their shoes were absolutely fabulous. They all looked as if they had never known that a war was going on. And here I was, in a very old cotton dress and sandals with clean, washed hair that cried out that it had not seen a hairdresser in a long time. I felt awful.

"Your father noticed that I got quieter all the time and asked me what was wrong. He had no idea that a woman could feel terrible under these circumstances. He thought I would be the happiest person there. Instead I was almost in tears. I finally told him what the problem was.

"He slapped his forehead and said, 'How could I have been so stupid! Of course, a woman's looks are important to her. I am so sorry to have brought you here, darling. I was just trying to make this a very happy occasion for both of us.' He looked so worried that I started to feel a little better. We finished our dinner, watched the dancers for a little while and then went home."

My mother smiled at me then, and I said, "I understand, Mom. Another time you will be the glamorous one!"

The next day my dad took her out to buy some new clothes and promised her a visit to a hairdresser soon. She was happy again.

CHAPTER EIGHTEEN

The Bridge on the River Kwai is the reality for my dad.

My dad was one of those unfortunate ones who had ended up working on the Burma Railroad. He was first transported to Surabaya, which was at the Eastern end of Java. Then he was sent to Semarang on the northern coast. From there he was sent to Bangkok and on to work on the infamous Burma Railway.

That is to say, about thirty-six to fifty percent of the civilian laborers and about one-quarter of the Allied prisoners of war died working on projects like the Bridge over the River Kwai, as the movie showed us.

My dad did not like to talk about those years, because it was too painful. He had been the representative for the group of Dutch military personnel among those Allied prisoners, but was soon chosen to represent all the Dutch civilian people as well, which made it even harder to accept all the atrocities that occurred. There was not much he was able to do to prevent them. Sick men were forced to work when it was obvious that they would collapse, but no protest by my dad was capable of stopping the Japanese overlords. "Work, work! No work, no eat!"

Now we can understand why many of the Japanese overlords were so severe; they had to work under very strict rules and on a very tight schedule. If they were late with a project it meant losing face. And that is something the Japanese find very hard to take, as I understand it. It just is not possible to lose face. I think that is about the worst that could happen, at least in those days.

I also think that is why the Japanese were so slow in accepting defeat, even after the first Atom bomb had fallen on Hiroshima. In the meantime, Russia had joined the Allied Forces. I think this fact may have been used by the Japanese to accept the surrender; that alone could have given them a real excuse. With Russia now against them as well, it was clear the war could not be won anymore. Even so, the second bomb on Nagasaki had to fall before the Japanese emperor finally decided to accept defeat.

CHAPTER NINETEEN

In which I learn to swim and can finally go down the water slide.

A week or so after our arrival in Bangkok, I found myself in a classroom with a group of other kids, aged from eight to sixteen. An attempt was made to start some kind of schooling for all of us, and this was the first time they got us together. The teacher explained what the idea was of putting us all in one classroom. She said that she was first going to tell us very general things that everybody should know about, so age was no problem.

She decided that the first thing she should do was to explain about what our planet Earth looked like, and she produced a globe. She said, "This is our planet. Here are the continents…"

At that point I was on my feet and I shouted, "Is the earth not flat?"

She said, "No, it really is round."

When I heard that I promptly started to cry. "Why did nobody tell me the earth was round? I was so afraid that we would fall of the edge all the time we were on the boat."

The teacher came to me and held me. She laughed a little and explained to all the others in the class that my experience was exactly what the old explorers, like Columbus, had experienced when they tried to sail around the world, not knowing for sure that it was round.

After a while I calmed down, but this was one lesson I was very happy to learn. Now, every time I am on a boat I stare at that dark line on the horizon and remember my fears and my agony. Growing up and learning about life was a tough job.

We enjoyed living in the compound with my dad. It was such a luxury for me to have a dad again. While he was working during the day I asked my mom if I could go into the pool that was there. All the kids were jumping in and sliding down the slide; it looked like so much fun. My mom was scared as I could not swim. She asked around and someone was ready to try and teach me. I went in the water and loved it, of course. After all those dreary years in the camps it was so nice to be surrounded by happy, laughing kids and smiling adults. After a week or so I was declared safe to go into the water but of course under supervision.

I had only one goal in my ten-year old life at that point—to go down that slide. I would feel so grown-up sliding down into the pool; it would be the most marvelous sensation I had ever had. "No, you are not ready yet. You must practice swimming just a bit longer." Oh, how I hated to be told to wait. Every day I swam and swam and I thought I was now most proficient in swimming. Finally, the day came that they told me, "Now you can go safely on the slide!"

My eyes sparkled and my whole body seemed to vibrate with anticipated excitement and pleasure. I climbed up to the top of the slide, sat down, and gazed at the water far below me. *Now*, I said to myself. *Go already*! I loosened my hands a little and slid down rapidly. I was a bit afraid because it was so much faster than I had anticipated, but I was happy too. I had finally made it to my goal. Then, just before I hit the water, something stung my right hand. I cried out and hit the water.

When I came up for air, I checked my right hand. It was all bloody, and I was told to get out of the pool so they could look after my hand.

What had happened?? Well, the pool and slide were old and with all the use it had gotten lately, the metal had gotten a bit loose and my hand had been cut right across my thumb. Result, I was covered in bandages and knew that I could not go into the pool anymore until I had healed. I cried myself to sleep that night.

This was not my last problem, though. I was, after all, a kid who had just lived through some very unpleasant camp years. I was still not up to what I should be and my immune system was still recovering. I caught a chill and developed pneumonia.

They sent me to the hospital. It was not far away and my parents came to see me every day, but it was very annoying. I still had head lice, and now I had to look after myself. I had a special comb that my mother had given me so that I could comb my hair to try and get rid of the little critters. I was so ashamed, hoping no one would know that I still had lice, so I diligently combed and combed and washed my hair every day when I was strong enough again. After a while I was considered cured enough to go home with my parents and I was thrilled. Now I could leave the dreaded hospital and my mom could look after me again. What a relief.

On the day I was going home I felt funny. Something was not right but I did not want to say anything to anyone; they might keep me longer in the hospital. I remember I walked between my parents, holding onto their hands. We walked through a little park and there were ducklings swimming in the pond. It looked so nice and peaceful, but I felt sicker and sicker. By the time I came home I was throwing up and running a fever. My parents were shocked and did not understand what was happening. I had just been declared cured; what was going on?

The doctor was called again and he looked me over. Throat, temperature, tummy, etc. Finally, he half-laughed and said, "Sorry to say, but your daughter has caught the measles in the hospital!" I did not think this was a laughing matter because it meant that I had to go back to the hospital again. I felt too sick to protest.

CHAPTER TWENTY

In which we move to a kampong and I get sick—again.

While I was in the hospital my parents decided they really wanted something more than a garage to live in so they started to look around for some more congenial living space. Nothing was available. Bangkok was overfull with returning soldiers and their families. Finally, they decided to rent a house in a nearby kampong (local village). The houses there were built on stilts, about three feet above the ground. The walls consisted of mattings only, but the house could be divided into two bedrooms, a living room, and a dining room. I think there was a kitchen upstairs as well, but I don't really remember exactly how it was.

It was nice and roomy and when I was at last brought to our new living quarters, I loved it. There were no other white people around to make me worry about whether they would find out my secret horror, the head lice, but only nice, brown children who were all ready to play with me. The spaces under the houses made for perfect play areas and I fondly remember the running around, laughing, and shouting for joy of those days. I never had a chance to go back to the pool and I certainly never went down the slide again, but by then that was okay.

I did go to some kind of school for a while. One day, some of the older kids in the school said they were going to see a movie at the theatre in town. The movie was called *Tarzan of the Apes*. I begged and cajoled my parents to let me go too and they finally relented. What an experience that was. It was Johnny Weissmuller who was playing Tarzan in those days. I thought he was magnificent. I never did get over my admiration for Tarzan, and even today I still watch Tarzan movies with great pleasure and glee.

But even these halcyon days came to an end. One day, my dad said that he was allowed to take a six-month leave and go to Holland with his family. We were to go on the ship called the *New Holland*. My father was in charge of the whole transport, which was a huge enterprise for him. Where to place all those families and women and children was an enormously challenging puzzle, but he was up for it. My dad could do anything!

Then the day came that we had to go aboard. My mom and dad and I came on board two days before the rest of the people because of all the figuring out my dad had to do. We did have a little cabin to ourselves, which was very nice. Of course, the whole ship had to be inspected from top to bottom and I happily traipsed along. The next morning, I woke up with a pain in my tummy that wouldn't go away. I asked my mom to let me stay in bed. She went upstairs to get some air.

After a while, the pain became really unbearable and I climbed out of bed. I found out that I could not stand upright, so I kind of crawled up the stairs to find my mom. She was shocked to see how much pain I was in and immediately called my dad. He in turn called the doctor to have a look at me. The doctor shook his head and said, "Sorry, but she's having an acute appendicitis attack and we must take her back to Bangkok. We do not have the facilities on board to do an operation like that."

My dad was aghast. "That is not possible. I am the organizer of this entire transport. I have to be on the ship. And I am not leaving my family behind here. There must be another solution."

There was another doctor on board and he was consulted. They decided to try an arrange an operating room and do the operation on the ship.

In the meantime, I was still lying in our cabin, waiting for the operation to happen. My dad came to sit with me and told me that we should pray to God to help us and take the pain away. My dad said that God would help me, but I did not believe him. "No, he won't." I said. "I am not Catholic and God is Catholic; he won't help me."

My dad was surprised. "Who says that?"

I then told him my whole story in between crying bouts from the pain.

He shook his head. "What utter nonsense. I could whip that nun! God helps us all, no matter who we are. Being Catholic or not has nothing to do with it. Just bow your head and pray with me."

I obediently bowed my head and prayed with my dad that God would take the pain away. Then my dad said, "While we are waiting for the doctors, why don't you close your eyes and try to sleep? I will stay here with you."

I closed my eyes and after some time, I did manage to fall asleep.

I slept for quite a while. Then the doctors came back to fetch me for the operation. My dad said that I was still asleep so they decided to let me sleep for a while longer. At last I woke up and said with a smile to my dad, "Daddy, I don't have a tummy ache anymore."

The doctors examined me closely and finally said, "She is right. There is no inflammation anymore. The appendix feels normal again."

They were really astonished that this could happen, but I said that God had healed me, just as my daddy said he would. They smiled at me and nodded their wise heads, but my dad kissed me and had tears in his eyes.

Then my mom could finally join us. She had been beside herself so my dad had told her to keep away from me, in order not to make me more upset than I was already. It was a happy reunion all over again. The family was still complete!

The doctors had warned my dad that the appendicitis could come back any time and we were very careful, looking for any signs of returning pains. The pains did not come back until 1953, and then I really had to get rid of my appendix.

CHAPTER TWENTY-ONE

In which I get a winter coat and meet the Keely-Keely man.

On the travel to Holland, several things happened that either made me very excited or very miserable. The first stop we made was in Bombay, a beautiful place full of life and color. We enjoyed walking around and looking at the beautiful plants and trees. I behaved admirably; no sickness, no tummy aches, no injuries. I was proud of myself.

Our next stop was in the Bay of Aqaba, between Jordan and Saudi-Arabia. Here they had set up huge tents on the coast in the desert where all our winter gear was displayed in all sizes. It was by now the end of May 1946. Coming from Indonesia and out of the camps we, of course, had no winter gear. Well, we did not have much of anything. As it was only the month of May, we were not too worried about that, but it had been decided that we should be supplied with needed winter gear. No-one had any money so the thought was really appreciated. I chose a winter coat of something prickly and red. It was supposed to be really warm.

It was terribly hot in the Red Sea but we managed. At least nobody was shooting at us and there were no rats or snakes or bugs to make our lives miserable. Then we came to Cairo. All I remember is a lot of people making a lot of noise, trying to get onto the ship, and muezzins calling from the minarets, telling the faithful that it was time for prayers to Allah, as my dad explained to me.

There was one man who gave a little show with baby chickens. I had never seen anything like it and was mesmerized. One moment there were none and suddenly they were running down his arms, or coming out of his pockets or from behind my ear! And every time he would shout, "Keely, Keely, Keely!"

It was lots of fun and I did not want to leave this spectacle, until my mother said, "Come on, Edie. We have to go back on board now. Don't you want to go to Holland?"

Oh, yes, I wanted to go to Holland; it was where I would meet my dad's brothers and my only grandmother and where it could be so cold in the winter that white stuff fell from the skies.

Many years later I was invited to go to a so-called tea-dance at a place called the "Champs Elysees" in the heart of downtown Amsterdam. One could order elaborate teas with all kinds of cakes and desserts, and in between, one could take to the dance floor. It was always really nice. They usually gave a small show in between the dances as well. This time, guess my delighted surprise when there appeared the Keely-Keely man. He had come a long way from Egypt. I sat back to enjoy his performance, and he did not disappoint. I was almost as impressed as I had been the first time I saw him.

CHAPTER TWENTY-TWO

In which I have to climb higher and higher to meet my grandmother and we move to my uncle's place.

And then there was the day that we had to get ready to disembark from the ship. Everybody was saying goodbye to everybody else, as did we. Then we stepped on shore in Amsterdam.

My grandmother lived on the third floor in a building right next to the Muiderpoort Station. That was her view. She had minimal living space, but where else could we go? Holland had also just come out of a terrible war and everything was still very expensive or not available at all yet. The door opened after we had pulled a bell. My parents let me go first, and I climbed to the first floor.

At the top of the stairs a door opened and a little old lady with white hair stood there with a big smile on her lips. "Welcome to Holland, little Edie!" she said.

I looked up at her and said shyly, "Hello Grandmother."

"Oh, no," the little old lady cried, "you have to go a little higher to find your grandmother."

I was abashed but obediently started to climb the second staircase.

Again, a door opened and another little old lady stood there with tears in her eyes. "Grandmother?" I said tentatively.

"No, no, I am your great-aunt Anna, your grandmother's sister."

By now I was frowning. What on earth was it with all these little old ladies? Where was my real grandmother?

Behind me, my mom and dad were laughing. My dad encouraged me to try the third staircase and up I went. This time when the door opened, there was another old lady but she was tall and she still had a lot of dark in her hair. She smiled, spread out her arms and hugged me, saying, "Finally I get to meet my little granddaughter, Edie! I have waited so long for this moment!" And then she too cried a little.

We now all went inside and my dad suddenly became a boy again. He had not seen his mother in twelve years and he too was overcome with emotion. I instantly liked my grandmother, and we became great friends. Later, I really admired her for her stamina, honesty, and courage. Except for the day when she announced that today we were going to finally have rice, for which I had begged her and begged her, as she was doing the cooking. My eyes lit up and I sat down to dinner with great expectations. All those potatoes, vegetables, and meat were dreadfully boring. I wanted my rice with Indonesian veggies and a bit of sambal (spice).

But when dinner came it was again potatoes with veggies and meatballs. I said, "Where is the rice, Grandma?"

"It's coming, it's coming," she said, smiling at me.

I thought that I would not have any room for the rice meal now, after eating the first dinner, but I sat back and waited.

Then she came into the room with a pudding—it was a RICE pudding!

I stared at it and was really upset with her. "But Grandma, that is not rice! That is just a pudding. I want rice as the main meal as we did back home."

Now my grandmother looked perplexed. She said apologetically, "I am so sorry, little Edie, I did not realize that was what you meant. But I don't know how to make such food. You must wait till your mama can cook it for you."

Then I took a deep breath, then another one, and finally managed to smile at her—I did love her a lot already—and I said, "It's okay, Grandma. Let's have the pudding now, shall we? Maybe I will like rice pudding too."

We soon settled down in Grandma's place. It was very cramped with the four of us, but apart from some nervous tensions left and right, we managed.

Then we moved to my dad's youngest brother's place; Uncle Kas. Uncle Kas and his wife, Jeanne, had given us their top floor where the bedrooms were. They kept the downstairs for themselves with the living and dining rooms, the kitchen, and a small bedroom where their two children slept. They themselves slept in the dining room. Their children, Karrie and Ria, were a few years younger than I was, but I soon loved them dearly. Aunt Jeanne was a wonderful and sweet woman. She and my uncle did everything in their power to make my mother feel comfortable. They even placed a piece of wood over the bathtub so that my mother could do her own cooking upstairs and feel really independent.

When winter started in Holland, and the canals froze, my dad decided that he would take me ice skating on the lakes and canals. He had an old pair of Friesian skates, which were very close to the ice and easy to use. He was so excited about being able to take his daughter ice skating! He put his old Friesians on and attached mine and showed me how to hold on to his hands. On the canals it was quite fun and I rather enjoyed it, but soon my unused muscles started to ache and the winter wind seemed to go right through my Aqaba coat.

It is not warm at all, I thought rebelliously. But my dad decided I had to do a turn on the lake as well, and there we went. I tentatively said, "Dad, don't you think this is enough for a first time? I am getting a little cold."

"No way," said my dad with a big smile on his face. "You are a Dutch girl and Dutch girls love to skate and go on the ice!"

"Oh," I said. "Okay then, we go on the lake."

We had the wind in our faces and were skating happily (my dad) and miserably (me). The wind became colder and colder and I skated slower and slower.

Finally, I cried out, "Dad, I want to go home now. I am COLD! I have never been so cold ever before!"

My dad looked at my poor face and red nose and finally relented. "All right then," he said. "Maybe this is enough for the day, eh?" I think that is when he started to remember that I had been born and raised in a tropical climate and maybe my body had not really adjusted yet to the cold temperatures of a Dutch winter.

I am sorry to say that he never managed to convince me again to go on the ice like a real Dutch girl.

In early November, my dad went back to Indonesia. My mom and I were to follow soon.

CHAPTER TWENTY-THREE

All about Mom's family and my first German Christmas.

One of the first things my mother wanted to do when we arrived in Holland was of course to visit her family in Germany. It was Christmas before we finally managed to visit the family at last.

Her oldest sister, Aunt Fitta (short for Elfriede) lived in Bochum in the so-called Ruhr District. The whole Ruhr District was known for its coal production. (My grandfather and uncle Heinz - aunt Fitta's husband - had both been mining engineers.) Uncle Heinz and my aunt Fitta had only been married for a few years when my grandmother died. My grandfather was totally left-handed in the house hold with eight children, and had little patience for everybody's problems. Chaos ensued. Aunt Fitta and uncle Heinz watched the proceedings for some time but then decided that they had to sacrifice themselves for the family. They moved in, and aunt Fitta ran the household. Soon everybody was starting to smile again and music was once more heard in the house.

Aunt Fitta and Uncle Heinz had two daughters. The oldest, whose name was also Elfriede, had been called Mausi when she was small, and Mausi she remained. She was five years older than I was. The youngest daughter was called Ingrid and she was almost six years younger than I was. We all got along great; I ran after Mausi, and Ingrid ran after me.

They lived in an apartment which was not very big, but they always managed to make the whole family feel welcome on any of their visits. In the kitchen there was an old-fashioned German Kuppersbusch wood-burning stove, which was always burning. A kettle for tea and coffee was always waiting, ready for use, and everybody would happily settle around the big table in the center of the kitchen. Uncle Heinz and aunt Fitta's bedroom was very big and had a huge, king-size bed. That is where most of us girls would sleep with my Aunt Fitta. All other guests were spread all over the apartment and nobody complained.

My mother could not wait to introduce me to their Christmas holiday customs. But first I had to meet my aunt Ella. She had arrived late in the evening so I had not met her. My mother brought her to where I was sleeping and woke me up. When I opened my eyes Mom said, giving me a big smile, "And this here is your aunt Ella about whom I have told you so many tales!"

I took one look at Aunt Ella, sat up, frowned, and said, "I don't like you!"

I spoke in Dutch, of course.

Aunt Ella turned to my mother and said, "Why is she mad at me, and what did she say?"

My mom asked me why I was saying that, and I replied, "She stole your beautiful new shoes and then you could not wear them anymore."

Mom started to laugh and explained to Aunt Ella that she had told me the story where Aunt Ella had "borrowed" my mom's new shoes and then given them back when they were completely out of shape from dancing too much on them.

Aunt Ella started to laugh, then, kneeling in front of me she said, "I will buy your mom new shoes today. Will you forgive me then?" I nodded shyly. She did buy my mom new shoes, for which my mom was very grateful and all was well again.

Everything else went fine; there were lots of cookies, the home-brewed wine passed from hand to hand, and everybody was in an excellent mood. On the 24th of December (German Heiligen Abend or Holy Night), all the grown-ups gathered around the big table in the dining room. Ingrid and I were considered too young to join in, but we sneaked a peek at the table. It was covered by a huge white tablecloth, but underneath were all kinds of parcels, apples, pears, chocolates, and I am sure the marzipan Scchweinchen (*little pigs made of marzipan—delicious*) would not be forgotten.

I did not understand why we were not allowed to join everybody else and was actually a bit miffed. I said to Ingrid, "Don't you think it is mean not to let us come in too?"

Ingrid, who was almost six at the time, just shrugged her shoulders and said, "I don't know why we can't come in too, but we can do lots of fun things here, you know. Mausi showed me where lots of goodies are hidden."

"Oh, goodies, all right. Let's go find those goodies, Ingrid."

And off we went. We did find lots of fun things to nibble on and things to play with, so we actually had a good time. We heard lots of rowdy sounds from the other room where the wine flowed freely, but it was just part of all the excitement of these days.

We had been told that we were allowed to call everybody at seven o'clock the next morning. Very early the next morning, Ingrid and I were ready to wake up the family. Once they had struggled out of their beds with sleepy eyes, we all wished each other a Blessed Christmas. Uncle Heinz, Aunt Fitta's husband, who had been forced to sleep on the too-short couch in the kitchen, was already up and the kettle was singing its early morning song. Soon there we were, "Oh, Tannenbaum," and a host of other dearly beloved Christmas songs sounding in the early Christmas morning, accompanied by Mausi on the piano. Then came the big moment—we would proceed to the table, which by then was again covered completely by a big white tablecloth.

Today I think that, funny enough, nobody actually mentioned Jesus as our Saviour, and how He died for us on the Cross—I wonder why not. All the people I met in those days did celebrate Christmas and Easter, but nobody really seemed to feel any real veneration for Christ. And neither did I, of course. That veneration did not come until very much later...

As soon as we were done singing, we all went to the table; Ingrid and I waiting with bated breath for the moment that the great big white tablecloth would be removed. Then we would see the whole table in all its splendor and glory with all the presents, wrapped (or rewrapped) beautifully in sparkling paper. And there it went! Ingrid and I ah-ed and oh-ed and finally took stock of what was really on that table.

First of all, there were all the big plates, filled with all kinds of goodies, like an apple, a marzipan Schweinchen or two, little toys, other fruit, and lots of small chocolate cookies and the like. Next to the plates were the presents, which the grown-ups had already seen the night before but had rewrapped, and there were more presents hanging from the knobs on the chairs.

I don't remember much of the actual presents, but this kind of Christmas was always the one I wanted to emulate in my later life. So much joy, so much happiness, and with really very little money. Nobody had much in those days just after the war, and the German people too had suffered great hardships and this Christmas the whole family wanted to make it special as it was the first one after the horrible war years, in which we all could be together again. Uncles and aunts and their children showed up during this Christmas holiday, and my mom had her fill of her beloved relatives.

And now we have to go back to my Uncle Kas and Aunt Jeanne's house and our lives there.

CHAPTER TWENTY-FOUR

In which I tangle with a Jewish girl and get quite resentful.

I went to school in the neighborhood of my uncle's house. They had put me in grade four, according to my age, but my knowledge was pitiful. I picked up fast, though, as I really enjoyed learning new things. Reading was always my greatest joy and I was soon the best reader in the class. My writing has always remained lamentable, though. I never knew whether to write straight up, in block letters, or curved, so I chose a mixture of the lot. And no matter what I did it never was a pretty sight.

I did become quite resentful of a girl in that last class before we went back to Indonesia. She was a Jewish girl, who sat right in front of me. She had long, black pigtails and everybody always excused anything wrong she did. If she had a tantrum, then they said, "Oh, her family went through so much during the war that her nerves are all shot." Holland had been very good at hiding Jews from the Germans during the war, I was told. I heard so many stories about this that I began to understand why everybody was indulging Rosie so much. She had lost quite a few relatives and when I heard that, I did begin to forgive her. But then I started to think that I, in Indonesia, had also had a very rough time, but nobody ever mentioned that.

We in the camps had suffered so much all those years, why did nobody ever talk about that?

Only much later did I discover that I was not the only one thinking like that. Other repatriates had also felt that Holland was not very sympathetic towards what had happened back in Indonesia. They had been so aware of the injustices done to the Jews all over Europe, as well as to themselves, that they spent little time considering that we in Indonesia had also had terrible times. They did not yet realize how many of us had died during these years because of all the deprivations we were put through.

I was happy when my mom told me that we were to embark at the beginning of January to go back to Indonesia. My dad had found our Aunt Suzy in Djakarta. She had a new man in her life, who owned a night club and she managed that night club for him. She lived above it. She wrote:

Dearest beloved pseudo daughter of mine!

It will be so wonderful to see you again, little Edie. I have missed you so much. That is why I went a little crazy about buying dresses for you! I have longed so often to put you into really nice clothes but we never had anything in the camps. Now I could indulge myself and I hope so much you will like them all...

She later added that she had also bought me lots of books to read. I was ecstatic and looked very much forward to seeing her again and to finding my presents. The dresses were indeed a dream come true. They were so beautiful that I cried for sheer joy. I was so happy to be 'home' again, and to being so spoiled, and to have Aunt Suzy back in my life, as well as my beloved dad. The next few years were very happy years.

CHAPTER TWENTY-FIVE

*In which we settle in nicely,
but I tangle with religion—again.*

We had been allotted living space in an old Chinese hotel in the older section of Djakarta. It was quite nice. Other colleagues of my dad were also stationed there and I really liked it. In the afternoon when everybody held a siesta hour, I would sneak outside the front gate. There usually was an old Chinese with a little stand, out of which he sold cold drinks with all kinds of delicious things floating in them. I loved them and bought myself a glass as often as I could. The old Chinese and I became good friends and he would always put a few extra goodies in my drink.

My parents had found a Roman Catholic school for me, which had a good reputation. I did not mind it too much. I just did not like to see the nuns; they reminded me too much of the nun who had reprimanded me so severely after my holy Communion. Also, I did not much like the priest who was teaching us religion. One day, he talked about Jesus and how Jesus went up on a cloud and disappeared from sight. I put up my hand and said, "That is not possible; he would fall right through it!" Yep, I was always very logical.

The whole class turned to me with open mouths as if I had said something really terrible. The priest got very angry. "You are a bad girl! *[Oh, oh, I knew that would come up again somehow.]* We should take every word that is written in the book of God as gospel. We do not doubt anything that is written in the Bible."

I bit my lips not to say anything more, but I thought rebelliously that it really was a very logical remark I had made; why couldn't he see that?

Today, at the ripe old age of eighty-three I look back on that day and still think the same way. All my life I have wanted to belief in my dad's God because he cured my appendicitis, but there were always things that just did not fit—that did not work for me. But my quest to find answers to this dilemma is a long and different story. So, back to my young self.

For me, the next few years were wonderful. We had a kokkie (cook), a babu choochi (she did the laundry, outside, of course) and a house boy to clean the house and serve the food. My mother was very happy. We had an ice box that needed a new piece of ice every Sunday. My dad and I would get up early and go get it. Most Sunday afternoons my parents would drop me off at the public swimming pool where I met my friends. We had a great time.

Aunt Suzy let me practice my piano lessons on the grand piano in the nightclub. In the afternoons there were always some hours that nobody was there. I would have to be sure to leave before a certain hour, though, as the Chinese community would come to play their gambling games. Once, I was late, and the faces of the gamblers showed their displeasure at seeing a child at the nightclub; gambling was a very serious business to them.

CHAPTER TWENTY-SIX

*In which the Dutch do a lot of fighting
and many people are killed.*

In the meantime, the so-called national War of Independence was still going on. There was constant fighting in many places, causing the Dutch regime a great deal of anxiety. The Dutch had come to Indonesia in the early 1600s in the shape of the Dutch East India Company to trade and buy goods. As had happened in India, the Dutch began to take more and more liberties and soon ruled the land. The Dutch East India Company stayed active in Indonesia till 1800. By then, the Dutch had established a military regime over the country which lasted till 1950.

Japan had occupied the country in early 1942 until August 1945. During this time many rebellious Indonesians who had been put in prison by the Dutch, like Ahmed Sukarno, had been liberated by the Japanese. Sukarno's cooperation with the Japanese did not just end with the need to acquire help to achieve independence; he even married a Japanese entertainer. I heard that he was a real womanizer, so that may not have been such a surprising thing. He now proceeded to foment strong anti-Dutch feelings amongst the population. As we had learned right after the war, Sukarno's slogan was, "Kill the white dogs!" His friend Hatta, who was a Dutch-educated lawyer was coldly intellectual, and more Dutch than Javanese in his outlook. Together, they formed an interesting partnership; the ideologue and the man of action, as an article said.

Just before the Japanese surrendered, Sukarno managed to declare Indonesia a republic on August 17, 1945. The next five years were chaotic. The Dutch sent 120,000 young men to help smother the rebellion. What happened next was not something the Dutch are proud of, I think. Around 100,000 Indonesian lives were lost in their fight for independence, as well as many thousands of Dutch, British, and Indian fighters.

"Owing to the young republic's tenacity, some sort of stalemate soon prevailed between the European armies (the Dutch and the British) garrisoned in the large cities, while the local rebels had free rein in the countryside. The fate of Madiun, in East Java, was interesting as it fell to hardcore communists, who were then crushed not by the Dutch but the budding republic's own troops.

In West Java a separate rising under the guise of *Darul Islam*, sought to wage jihad and establish a grand theocracy, which lasted two decades. (Jihad means waging war against the enemies of Islam.) The Darul Islam was an Islamist group that fought for the establishment of an Islamic state in Indonesia. It was established in 1942 by a group of Muslim militias, which recognised only *Shari'a* as a valid source of law.

Even the Japanese had a role in the conflict. With a substantial garrison stuck in Java, IJA (Imperial Japanese Army) officers willingly lent arms and equipment to the Indonesian resistance before departing for their homeland. This was done just as the British were relying on Japanese troops to help police the restive colony.[5]

In the end, it was not so much Sukarno who was victorious but the United Nations, who decided to recognize Indonesia's independence on 27 December, 1949. The Dutch reluctantly acquiesced because they realized that this was a sign of the times. More and more subdued nations were fighting their own wars for independence, like the Vietnamese and Algerians against the French, The Congo nation against the Belgians, and the Palestinians against the British, etc.

---

[5] Miguel Miranda explains the anti-colonial movement and quest for independence in post-World War Two Indonesia.) From the website of www.historyisnowmagazine.com

CHAPTER TWENTY-SEVEN

In which I spend four happy years in Batavia, followed by the final heart-wrenching good-bye to the beloved country of my birth.

While all these political events were taking place, I was spending happy times in Batavia. Our servants seemed to love me and spoil me more than my parents. And I loved them. Later on, when I was a bit older, I went to school on my beautiful Fongers bike (a present from Aunt Suzy, of course) and never worried that anything could happen to me. I had nice friends and even almost got elected to class rep. The boy that won even told me he had voted for me. What a triumph.

I did have a big handicap—I was chubby. And so was my best friend, Mick. She was small and round and I was tall and, yes, there is no better word for it: chubby. Nobody would choose us when we had to play games outside, but we understood that. We knew that we just could not outrun anybody, so we would swallow our pride and just shrug our shoulders. The kids in our class were quite accepting of us, though. I guess because Mick was (and is) a really nice person and I guess they could tolerate me. Mick and I are still great friends today. She is still small and round and I am still tall and...on the chubby side, although I do try hard not to get really fat.

Being chubby as a young girl is very, very hard. One wants to be as slim and pretty as the girls that have slews of boys running after them. We think it is because they are so slim. It does have something to do with it, of course, but for the most part it is because this gives the girls confidence. They dare to show their sexuality because they know the boys like them. When you are chubby, you are inclined to think that you don't have any of that important sexuality. It is not true, but it is hard to convince a chubby young girl about this. In short, being chubby is not easy when you are a teenager. If only teenagers could realize that it is not size that matters but personality. How much easier life would be then.

Mick and I had gone to the Dutch high school, called "The Carpentier Alting Stichting." I really enjoyed almost all my classes, except for botany. That was to me so incredibly boring that I would yawn my way through each class. Today I am very sorry that was the case. The lives of plants, trees, and anything that lives and grows is so fascinating. To think that all of that is so closely connected to ourselves. We have cells—they have cells. We have feelings—they have feelings. They need to be nurtured carefully, as do we ourselves. There are just a few differences between us, but we get our genes and our lives from the very same source: nature. Nature is in all of us and everywhere. Whatever nature does affects us all. I think I need another lifetime to learn more about all the important things.

My dad knew that his days in Djakarta were numbered. With Indonesia now an independent republic, there was no more need for Dutch military personnel to be stationed there, and the Indonesians were practically pushing anyone Dutch out of the country. It must have been very hard for anyone who had spent so many years there and almost considered it his or her own country, to know that they were now personae non-grata (unwelcome people).

So, when my dad told us that we were going to board the "Cheshire" on the 15th of May, 1950 we were resigned to our fate. We would have to start life over in Holland somehow. I would have to find a boarding school of some kind, and my dad had no idea what he was going to do after coming back to live in his own country. I did not want to leave to go to cold Holland. I wanted to stay right where we were and go to school with my friends and go to the pool every Sunday. They had now instituted a dance band to play during the afternoons at the pool side, and all of us were very excited at the prospect. Who would voluntarily want to leave now? I hated to say goodbye to our servants and they all cried when we left, as did we.

Aunt Suzy brought us to the ship and promised to write often and to try and come to Holland as soon as she could. Mick and I had said goodbye earlier, and that was really hard. When would we be able to see each other again?

And there was the whistle. Everyone who was not a passenger had to leave the ship. More goodbyes were said, and then they left. Music was playing on the quay and everyone waved and waved. Few people looked happy but many were openly crying. And then we slowly distanced ourselves from the coast and tried not to cry too hard. That was the last time I saw 'my' country; the place I was born in and where I had spent most of my life. It felt like it was an end to a very important era.

CHAPTER TWENTY-EIGHT

In which my dad gets very hurt and ends up abandoning Holland.

When we arrived in Holland, we had to travel to somewhere in the country where the army had found a place that could accommodate many of the repatriating army personnel and their families. It was make-shift at best and certainly no solution, so we ended up staying with my grandmother again. I was happy to be there and to see her, but now I know that nerves were frayed because my dad did not know what was going to happen. In Holland, a man who had not finished high school could not become an officer. My dad had reached the highest rank available for him, that of under-lieutenant, but now that there was no longer a colony to go to, everything had changed.

My dad asked them to give him a job as a non-military person, with the same pay as a higher-ranked officer would get. He felt that everything he had done throughout the war should enable them to give him some preferential treatment. He waited for the answer to his request week after week. At last the letter came—no, they could not give him what he had asked for. It just was not in the books to give anyone preferential treatment. They did offer him an office job, but would not increase his pay above the level of under-lieutenant.

My dad was so hurt that they were not ready to even acknowledge what he had done during the terrible war years, that he had a nervous break-down. I was hiding in a corner somewhere and watched him thrashing his heels on the floor and crying harsh sobs for a long time. My grandmother did not know what to do to help him, and my mother cried along with my dad. It was a horrible time for all of us.

In the weeks that followed, my dad read all the ads in the newspapers he could find, and one day he came home to Grandma's place and said, "We are going to Turkey!"

"What? How come? Why? Are we all going?" The questions flew around and then he told us what he had done. A Dutch company called, "Royal Netherlands Harbour Works Company" had advertised for a stock manager at a small harbour they were building in the Bay of Izmit near Istanbul. He would be in charge of all the stock and the import and export again of all the stock, including dredgers, cranes, etc. The pay was not high but would increase if he could prove himself to be a valuable man in this job.

There was silence for a few moments while we all tried to digest what he had told us. Then my mother asked tentatively, "And what about your army career?"

My dad laughed disdainfully. "What career? I have had it with the army. They can't hurt me anymore."

They decided to take me with them and have me take correspondence lessons instead of going to school. My mom was nervous because the Korean War was going on; she was afraid it would result in another world war, and she wanted to keep both of us close to her. My dad finally agreed, and within two weeks we said goodbye again to my grandmother and were on our way to the airport to fly to Istanbul. My grandmother had given my dad some mail that had arrived just before we left, and he now opened the first letter. It was from Army Headquarters; they wrote that they had re-evaluated the whole war scenario and my dad's role in it, and they had finally decided to accept his proposal after all. He would get the higher pay and do so in a civilian role. In fact, they accepted everything my dad had asked for...

My dad's reaction? "Damn, damn, damn! Why couldn't they have done it sooner!" Then: "And why did I act in such haste?!"

Yes, why did he? Kismet, as the Turks say. It is fate. In time, my dad as well as my mom learned to accept that this was what was meant to happen. Today, I think that maybe in another parallel universe, my dad had not seen the Turkey job ad. He had received the letter from the army and had happily accepted the new position at headquarters. I wish I could have just a little peek to see what would have happened then to all of us.

CHAPTER TWENTY-NINE

In which my dad is told off by a Turk, threatens a dentist, and I scream the place down.

Flying in a big airplane was a new experience, and every time the plane dropped a little, I was scared that we were going down, but we arrived safely at Istanbul Airport. It was colorful, busy, confusing, and LOUD!

(Quite recently I went back to Istanbul with a friend of mine. She was terrified when we arrived at the airport. "Is there a revolution going on? Why are they fighting? Who is actually fighting?"

I soon calmed her down. "Don't worry, Ann. They are always like this; it's the Turkish way!")

We stayed a night in a nice hotel in Old Istanbul and continued by train the next day to our next destination; Izmit in the Gulf of Izmit.

Izmit turned out to be a small town on the north side of the bay with a population of around 36,000. (Today it is close to 400,000). It has a sub-tropical climate, although it can get quite cool in the winter months. Golcuk, our final destination, was on the south side of the bay. We had to take a boat to get there.

What I did not know at the time was that the small town of Izmit had already existed a very long time. They actually go back to 712 BC. In antiquity, the city in was called Astacus or Olbia, in Greek. After being destroyed, it was rebuilt by Nicomedes I of Bithynia in 264 BC and given the name of Nicomedia. It remained one of the most important cities in northwestern Asia Minor. When I was there, I would have found it hard to believe that this little insignificant place once had been the metropolis of Bithynia under the Roman Empire, and that Emperor Diocletion made it the eastern capital city of the Roman Empire in AD 286.

Later, I also found out that, in nearby Getzethe, hero Hannibal of Carthage, who fought Rome by taking forty elephants and an army across the Alps, came to Nicomedia in his final years to commit suicide, because his father had made him swear by a blood oath as a very young boy to never, ever surrender to the Romans. They had been close to capturing him when he killed himself.

During my retirement, I had been teaching Ancient Civilizations for seventeen years at the Society for Learning in Retirement. In one of my last classes I told them the history of Hannibal—how he had been incredibly brave in his attempt to conquer Rome by taking those forty elephants and a large army across the Alps. At the end of that class someone asked, "How many elephants survived?" Even though it had been thousands of years before our own era I still had tears in my eyes when I replied, "Just one..."

Okay, okay, back to my young self! But for someone who loves ancient history as much as I do, there are few things more exciting than to think of what went on long before I stepped on those very same stones.

We were taken to our new home; an apartment in a block of four a few miles away from the harbor section of the town. My dad had a jeep for transport, so we were free to explore the surroundings. We liked it there. I was thrilled to see that the Mediterranean was really and truly as blue as they had promised me.

One day I had to go see a dentist. There were none in Golcuk so we had to cross by the same boat back to Izmit, where there was supposed to be a good dentist. My mother took me there. The problem was a milk tooth on the upper left front. It stubbornly stayed in place while the real tooth was growing behind it, not finding enough room. I had to get rid of the milk tooth. It seemed a simple enough problem.

We were welcomed by the dentist and I was seated in the dentist's chair. As I looked across him, I noticed that the door was wide open and a lot of Turkish women were trying to see what the dentist was going to do to me. Also, in the window many faces peered inside. I guess they had never seen someone like me being treated, so it was a great occasion for them. The dentist most probably told everyone that this European girl was going to be treated, and they were all here to cheer him on. And there they were, happily anticipating events to come.

I was determined not to show any sign of fear, but in my heart, I was really scared. My faith in the dentist's ability to treat me properly was not very high. I got an injection to kill the pain and survived that part. So far, so good. While waiting for the painkiller to take effect, the dentist was talking up a storm to my mother, who, naturally, did not understand a word of what he was saying. She bravely nodded from time to time to show that she was with him.

Then came the extraction part. He pulled and pulled, then pulled again. I thought, why is he pulling so often? I heard something clinking in a bowl and then something else going into the bowl. What was he doing?

I rinsed and rinsed my mouth afterwards and then looked into the bowl. I saw two teeth lying in the bowl. I then looked around for a mirror, found one and looked at my mouth. I had a huge big hole where my real tooth should have been. The idiot had pulled BOTH teeth! I screamed from sheer shock. All the people around us had been ready to congratulate the dentist on a job well-done. They now did not know what to think of my reaction.

My mother nearly pummeled the dentist to a pulp, yelling her own opinion to him, pointing at the second tooth. She kept gesticulating, and shouting "No, no, no!" pointing at the second tooth, and finally he seemed to get it. He became very apologetic and seemed to say a whole lot to us, which we again did not understand. We left, amid a crowd which stared at us in confusion; they had been so ready to cheer.

The next day, my dad went to see the dentist. This time he had an interpreter with him (which is what we should have done, I guess, but who would have thought that he would not understand that only the milk tooth had to be pulled?) The dentist promised to have a false tooth ready pronto and would make me beautiful again. My dad had told him how I was so upset because now I looked so ugly and no young man would look at me like this. That was something the dentist could well understand. It was hard to get rid of daughters, especially if you had no good dowry to give them.

I read the other day that "Izmit may become Turkey's second Ephesus," because after the last earthquake in 1999 (in which 17,000 people died) it was discovered during removal of the debris that a large city with a huge palace had existed right underneath. Many great artifacts were discovered and archaeologists were very excited to start officially excavating. It is unbelievable that nobody had ever thought that this might be the case. The whole of Turkey is one archaeological paradise! Oh, if only I could go back and live my life again, knowing what I know now! My little dentist could have been living right on top of the ancient palace of a Roman emperor. If only he had been a little more enterprising and had started digging in his backyard, he could have been the one to find the giant sculpture of Heracles...

CHAPTER THIRTY

In which my mother gets a job and the cook wiggles his thumbs in his ears.

There were a few bachelors in the other apartment across the hall from us, as well as a young married couple, Nick and Holly. Nick was an engineer from Delft University in Holland. My mom was asked, after a few weeks, whether she would mind looking after the bachelors in the other apartment. There was a Turkish cook but he needed supervision. My mom agreed to supervise. Then she went down to find the young cook to see how they could communicate. He knew a few words of English, but other than that he just knew his own language: Turkish. My mom had a crash course in Turkish when 'discussing' menus. Somehow, they managed to get the messages across and everybody was pleased that the food was better.

One day, my mom went to talk to the cook again, but when she came to the kitchen there was no cook to be found anywhere. She walked around and decided to wait a while—maybe he was just delayed by something. Finally, he arrived with a big smile on his face. My mom frowned and asked him why he was late by pointing at her watch. Then something strange happened. He stuck both thumbs in his ears and bowed up and down. Then he smiled again as if that was enough explanation.

She had no idea what it could mean and let it go. When she mentioned it to my dad he started to laugh. "Oh, woman, haven't you learned that yet? He went to pray at the mosque. There are prayer mats at the mosque on which the believers can kneel and then bow down till they almost touch the carpet with their noses. Their hands are then next to their faces and that was what he was trying to tell you."

Now my mom laughed and said, "Learned something new again!"

My dad was quickly adapting to the new job and seemed to enjoy it. He was learning Turkish at a good pace, but was often too impatient to try to remember the names of all the workers. He had the habit of calling them all "Jansen" in Dutch (Johnson). "Hey, Jansen, come here," he would say, while beckoning with his hand.

This seemed to work well for him, but one day a Turk answered in German, "Aber Herr Schmidt, ich heisz doch kein Janzen!" (*But Mr. Smidt, you know Jansen is not my name!*)

My dad did a double-take and hastily apologized. "So sorry, my thoughts were somewhere else." After that he was a bit more careful as how to address the Turkish personnel.

CHAPTER THIRTY-ONE

In which I go to a wrestling match and get kissed—yak!

There were quite a few Turkish government officials involved with the building of the little harbour. They were there to see to it that our company stuck to all the agreements and was not costing the government more than necessary. The relationship between the Turkish officials and the Dutch personnel was quite good. There was one man in particular who really enjoyed it when my mother played the piano at parties and sang her lovely songs. His name was Enver Bekir. One day he said to my parents, "I am going away for a few days to Istanbul to visit my wife. Why don't I take your daughter along so she can see something of Istanbul?" After some discussion they agreed. I had visions of being taken to a dance or two, or even just having nice dinners in beautiful places.

Now I think that they were crazy to let their fifteen-year-old daughter go alone to a town like Istanbul with a man who was old enough to be her father, but virile enough to still have an eye for someone young and new. However, I went with him and the train travel to Istanbul was quite interesting. He tried to explain what we were seeing and behaved like a gentleman.

We came to his house and I met his wife. She was not too thrilled to see him come back with a young girl in tow, and I did not blame her. I realized then in what an awkward situation Enver Bekir had placed me. However, I was there and I had to make the best of it. I tried to be as unobtrusive as I could but still, they had to take account of me; I was a guest, after all. What I also did not know was that both Enver and his wife were great wrestling fans.

Since then I have discovered that wrestling is almost the national sport in Turkey, so it was not surprising that this couple were fans. Enver's wife had managed to get tickets to a wrestling match that was going on that very evening and Enver was very pleased. But what to do with me? They finally decided to try and get another ticket and to take me to the match. I thought, *Wrestling? Oh, no!* Oh yes, we all went, Enver happily explaining to me how lucky I was to get to see such a great match.

I saw the first two men and shuddered; it was not a pretty sight. They were so big and so fat and wore only some kind of clothing on their most private parts. The rest was bare and shiny because they doused their bodies in oil. Then they suddenly banged into each other, and... No, I don't want to explain the rest. I was not pleased, that was definite. Enver and his wife were shouting and clapping throughout every match; they just really enjoyed themselves. I was trying not to show too much that I really loathed what I was seeing. Well, don't blame me; wrestling is not for everyone. When it was all over after many hours, I was hoping that they would take me out to supper somewhere exciting, but no, we went straight home. We had something to eat and went straight to bed.

The next morning, we had breakfast and I was hoping we would go somewhere where I could be happy too. I don't even remember what we did the rest of that day, but I vividly remember what happened in-between. Enver caught me alone in the dining room, grabbed me in his arms, and proceeded to kiss me deeply. I struggled, of course, but to no avail. I had never been kissed before and had no idea a kiss could be so awful. Enver was very pleased with himself, though, and smiled all day long.

We went home the next day, and I was very happy to see my parents again. I did not dare tell them what Enver had done. My mother was always so pleased when Enver asked her to sing and play at the occasional parties, that I did not want to spoil that for her. She seemed to be so happy these days, and she certainly deserved some pleasure now and then, after all the difficult times she had had in her life.

CHAPTER THIRTY-TWO

In which I meet up with a big snake and fall fatefully and hopelessly in love.

Me at 15 years old.

My dad had applied for a high school correspondence course in my grade, and I was put to work every day. In our free time we would go to the beach and swim and enjoy the sunshine. That is also when I started to play tennis, which became a life-long passion. Sometimes whole groups of us from the

Harbourworks company would go on picnics in the countryside. On one occasion we camped down near a ruin of one of those old crusader castles. What we did not know was that there were lots of snakes in the area, big ones as well as small ones. We were camped near a very dense forest and when the need arose, we would just walk away from the others, go into the forest, do our thing, and go back to the site.

No one had a problem, but then came my turn. On the way back, I was happily traipsing along when suddenly this huge snake stood in front of me. I was momentarily paralyzed with shock, but then I realized I had to do something. That monster was ready to eat me, I thought, and so I screamed my head off. The screams must have hurt the snake's ears for he turned away and disappeared into the bushes. The others heard me as well and came running through the trees towards me. "What is the matter? What happened? Are you all right?" I burst into tears, more from shock than from anything else, and explained what had happened. They oh'ed and ah'ed and consoled me and soon afterwards we left to go back home. What was it with snakes; did they have it in for me?

Sometime later, we were told that a big viper had attacked a man who was sightseeing at the castle. He had not managed to escape. When I heard that, I was very happy to be alive! The snake I saw probably was the big black snake, which is not very dangerous, but certainly very scary. At least, I think it might have been, but I am still not sure.

My studies in most subjects went quite well, but my math was not easy. Everybody was so busy, nobody seemed to have time to explain things to me. Then one of the bachelors, Jack, said he would not mind helping me out. I was thrilled. Jack was in his late twenties and quite good-looking. I was fifteen years old and discovering that I was a woman, albeit a very young one. I had even been kissed already, although that was not an experience I wanted to repeat. Jack was a great help with my math; my problem was that I fell hopelessly in love with him. I was really quite innocent and barely knew where babies came from yet. I was prepared to admire Jack from a distance, so to speak, as I had no illusions that he would ever return my feelings.

Things continued for a while with nothing special happening. Then one day he lightly stroked my arm. I was tingling all over and looked at him. He looked back at me and smiled. We continued with the math problem. After this little episode he slowly increased his little attentions. I knew I should tell my parents about this, but my hormones were raging. I was waking up to all these new feelings; I did not want it to stop. Then, one day he put his arm around me and kissed me. Now this was how a kiss should feel—I was ecstatic. He did return my feelings; how wonderful. I immediately wondered how he would behave to me tomorrow, so I asked, "How will you be tomorrow, Mr. Baker?"

Yes, I addressed him as a child to an adult. He withdrew his arm and said derogatively, "How would I know that?" I was hurt, but then decided that I should be happy that he had kissed me at least once. I courageously returned to my math problem as if nothing special had occurred.

The next time I went to his room with my homework we just did math. I was disappointed but kept hoping he would kiss me again some time. And a few days later he did. He was more passionate this time and said, "We will have to do something about this situation one of these days." I was excited and happy and floated through the next few days. He kissed me now every time I showed up, and started to caress me more intimately. I was worried and scared, but so happy with all these exciting feelings coursing through my body. And then it happened.

CHAPTER THIRTY-THREE

In which I fall more in love and finally really become a very bad girl.

Mr. Baker said we should see each other when everybody had gone to bed. I thought he would come to my room across the balcony, but he said no, that would not be a good idea. My parents' room was too close to mine. I should climb across our balcony to his. It was only a short step and should not give me any problem. I did not like the idea; heights had never appealed to me much. However, to be alone with him I was ready to do it. And so, one night, I climbed across the balconies and he pulled me into his room. That night he did not just caress me. He undressed me very deliberately. Did I like it? I was scared, I did not know where this would lead. I should have stopped him, but he was the adult. I was just a very stupid young girl who thought she was in love. I wanted him to go on, but I also wanted to run home and be safe. I did not say anything, but let him do what he wanted to do. He caressed my naked body briefly, and then got on top of me. I was really worried by now—what was he doing? What was going on?

Then he was inside of me and I cried out; it was painful and I did not like it. It got worse and again I cried out. He shushed me and continued with what he was doing. It did not last long and then I was free again.

Instead of explaining to me what had happened, he proceeded to tell me that he had had much nicer and longer sessions with his previous girlfriend. All I had wanted was to please him, so he would go on kissing me and paying attention to me. He continued saying things like how his previous girlfriend had been able to 'entertain' him so much better. I felt guilty. I thought it must have been my fault; that I had done something terribly wrong.

Looking back, I realize he must have felt angry at himself for having been ready so quickly. He never did show any real affection for me. I now realize that, being a bachelor and not meeting any women he could have any kind of relationship with, it must have been tempting to start something with a young girl, who so obviously was infatuated with him. My parents never clued in, but some of the others must have had some idea about how he behaved towards me, because one of them said to my parents, "You should send your daughter back to Holland to go to school there. This life is not good for her. She is the only child among all these adults."

This did make my parents think. Then they told me they had decided to send me to a boarding school in Holland come September. I was not pleased with this idea but had to accept it. I did hug the knowledge to myself, though, that I still had several months to be with Jack Baker sometimes. He often acted as if he was just my teacher, never touching me or kissing me or saying anything about our situation at all. It was very frustrating, but I was hoping every time I saw him that he would kiss me again, or let me know he wanted to see me again.

He did finally tell me it was time for another trip across the balcony. I complied, not surprisingly, with alacrity. The first thing he told me was how upset he had been the first time, as his sheet got all bloody.

"Why did it get all bloody?" I asked.

He scowled at me, "Because I took your virginity, stupid." I still did not understand why that would cause the bleeding, but as usual I apologized. He just smirked.

I told myself it showed that he cared for me, that he still wanted to see me, but he never said one kind thing to me. This was very hard to take, but I felt very humble because I was not even sixteen years old yet and did not really know how to 'entertain' a man like him. This situation continued until my departure. He made me do one or two more trips over the balcony.

Sometime later, my parents did discover somehow what had happened. They were furious with Jack Baker, as well as with me. And right they were. I had truly become a very bad girl, just as the nun had told me.

And Jack? Today he would have been put behind bars for 'seducing a minor', but at that time those ideas had not quite materialized yet. I had behaved as badly as he had. One should not have sex before marriage, and I had known that. I just hadn't known what 'having sex' implied. My mother had bought me a little book on sex, which talked a lot about the birds and the bees, but never taught me how to disregard those sexual feelings that are so difficult to deal with in a young girl's life. Or in any young person's life. Not having any friends other than the adults around me also was a difficult thing. I really felt very lonely most of the time. My parents had each other—everyone seemed to have someone in their lives. Everyone but me. Is this a good excuse for my behavior? No, nothing excused my behavior. I knew that what I was doing was wrong. But I was so desperate to 'belong' to someone that I ignored all those wise words that coursed through my brain.

I just rediscovered a group I used to love to listen and dance to when I was young. They were singing a song called "Georgie," which ends heartbreakingly with words like "Please love me." That is how I felt at that time. I never dared to say it to Jack, but I thought it over and over again—please, love me just a little.

CHAPTER THIRTY-FOUR

In which a Turkish young man wants to buy me, and I tangle again with religion.

Towards the end of my stay with my parents in Golcuk, there was an interesting episode. One of my dad's Turkish men had thrown me many looks for some time. I just thought he found me a strange girl as the Turkish girls were so different from what I looked like and how I behaved. However, one day he asked to speak to my dad. He said that he was very interested in me and offered to buy me, so he could marry me. My dad was completely surprised, to say the least. His first instinct was to start laughing, but then he realized that the young man was very serious and anxious. He just said, "I am happy you like my daughter, but she is too young. She is only fifteen years old."

Then the young man said, "But that is the right age for a girl to get married. I have saved up quite a bit for my marriage and I can pay you 5000 Turkish Lira (dollar)."

"Oh," said my dad, "that is a lot of money, but I don't want her to get married yet. I think she is too young."

The young man thought deeply for a moment and then said, "You know what? I will give you a camel as well as the money. I really want to marry her." My dad told him that it was a very generous offer but the answer was still no. Shaking his head at my dad's refusal to let him marry me, the young man left the office with a sad face. When my father told my mother and myself the story later, I felt a little comforted by it. At least somebody seemed to love me!

So, I went to boarding school where I was very happy to realize that I was not too far behind everyone else. I did not like to be there, though. I was a person who liked to curl up in a comfortable chair and read, and who liked the warmth from knowing my parents did love me, after all. The whole being at home idea was what I craved. The strict regime at the school was anathema to me.

Religion caused problems again. I knew now that I was Protestant and not Catholic, but apparently there were two different kinds of Protestant groups as well. One kind went to church once on a Sunday and the other kind went twice. Guess which kind I chose to be! I still was not comfortable being in a church. That nun had really scared me! Once, I decided to say that I was not feeling very well and did not want to go. The headmistress said immediately, "Oh, that is fine. You can sit with me while I listen to a radio service." Yeah, what a great idea! Yes, that was my punishment!

My last year in high school was spent with a nice family in Hilversum, which lies in the heart of Holland. My parents had listened to my pleas and found this wonderful place. I enjoyed living with a family in a home atmosphere, and I also liked the school I went to. I was still chubby but no one ever said anything derogatory to me. Maybe the fact that I came all the way from Turkey had something to do with it. It may have given me a bit of an exotic aura, who knows? I also had a very nice friend now. Her name was Ria Lock. She and I became great pals.

One day, I had a terrible tummy ache while in our history class. I finally could not stand it anymore and I said, "May I be excused? I have a very bad tummy ache."

The teacher looked at me and said, "Young lady, by now you should be used to getting tummy aches; just wait till the end of the class."

I waited but it was agony. After class, Ria and I went to see the principal. I explained my problem and the principal immediately told me to go home. I could not ride my bike, it was too painful, but Ria took me behind her on the bike and pedaled me home.

Aunt Akke, the sister of Aunt Nel, who ran the household, called the doctor. By now I was whimpering and crying, huddled on the couch in the living room and covered by a blanket with a heating pad on my stomach.

The doctor came. It did not take long to make a diagnosis. "It is acute appendicitis. She needs to be operated on immediately."

By eight o'clock that night I had been operated upon and was lying comfortably in my hospital bed. Guess who was my very first visitor the next day? You are right—my history teacher. He apologized profusely and begged me to forgive him for being so insensitive. I laughed. "It is all right. You probably get a lot of silly excuses from students all the time".

But I was very happy that he had come. It had cost me a lot of extra pain having to stay in the class.

I did my finals in the month of June and found I had succeeded in doing quite well, especially in the language department. In math I only achieved two sevens (out of ten) but that was good enough for me. I had decided that I was going to a secretarial school for two years where I was supposed to study four languages, including stenography, in all of them, as well as learn how to run an office most efficiently. I liked office work. In Golcuk I had often helped in the office when needed. I would have been able to achieve a prestigious secretarial position, which really appealed to me, and would have been paid well.

However, man proposes, but Someone up there often has different ideas. After three weeks of studying I received a telegram from my father. "Have enough of being alone. Drop everything and come."

I was very enterprising so, nothing daunted, I was in Istanbul three days later. There I had to wait for a ship to take me around to Zonguldak on Turkey's northern border on the Black Sea. It was an overnight trip. We arrived around noon the next day. I shared the cabin with a nice lady with whom I also had dinner. She said her name was Eugenie Lavroff. She seemed to me a bit stand-offish, but I did not really care. If I had known what was going to happen, I would have studied her much more closely!

My parents were there to receive me, and I was kissed and hugged thoroughly by both Mom and Dad. I was so pleased to see them. The lady from my cabin was greeted much more reservedly by a gentleman in his forties in the most awful Hawaiian shirt I had ever seen. When we were introduced to each other we looked into each other's eyes and something seemed to spring up between us. It was an ephemeral moment, soon mostly forgotten in the excitement of being again in Turkey. We each went our own way, and my parents and I talked all the way to my new home about everything and nothing. I did turn around once to have another look at the other couple. I felt a vague disappointment that they were not coming in our car as well. And I don't think it was because I liked her so much...

PART 2: THE GROWN UP YEARS

CHAPTER THIRTY-FIVE

In which Dad finds me a job, and I have to write a letter in shorthand, dictated in French, both of which I am not yet capable of.

Me at 17 years old.

Well, there I was. Seventeen years old and no job experience or special knowledge of any kind. "What shall I do here?" I asked myself. All I could do quite well was typing; that much I had already picked up at my course. I had also started to do stenography in the Dutch language but a few lessons won't make you a star!

That night at dinner we talked about it. My father said, "I think you can get a job at the office. Our secretary is leaving as this is almost the end of this particular job (the building of a coal harbor), and they may want somebody to type the Dutch letters.

*Hmm...*I thought, *that might not be a bad idea. Office work I can probably handle.* The next day Dad came home and said triumphantly, "They agreed that they could use somebody; you are hired! "

"Whoopee! Thank you, Dad. I am so pleased that you managed to get me a job!"

The next morning, I was driven with several other employees to the office at the site. The Dutch secretary who was going to leave at the end of the week showed me around, explained things to me about the running of the office, and told me not to be afraid when the agent called me to dictate a letter. The agent had been in charge of the construction of this harbor but was also leaving in a few months' time. The secretary said, "He dictates very slowly, but unfortunately often changes his mind about how he wants to word it!"

I did not much like the sound of that. After all, I still could not do any shorthand. A very short time later there was a call from the agent. "I need to dictate a letter."

The secretary looked at me. "This is a good occasion for you to do this. I can help you afterwards to explain what he meant to say."

Okay. With trembling knees I knocked on the boss's door and went in. There I saw an older gentleman behind his desk, who looked distracted. He saw me. "Who are you?"

"I am your new secretary, Edith Smidt, as Miss Heemstra is leaving at the end of the week."

His face cleared up. "Oh, good. Well, sit down." And then began the nightmare.

He started: "Messieurs, Je vous remercie pour votre lettre de Juin..."

I interfered with a fluttering heart. "Sorry, sir, but I don't know French stenography."

He frowned, then his expression lifted. "But I'll speak slowly, so you can just write it down."

I nodded my head, loath to tell him that my French was not very good either. I had learned French in school, but how much French is that? Anyway, I wrote down what he said, but writing down was not the problem. The problem was the way he dictated. There came a full sentence of which he seemed very proud. He beamed at me, but I didn't beam back. He had lost me after the first five words...*Ouch*. I timidly asked, "Could you repeat that last part, sir?"

"No, of course not!" he shouted.

Well, we both struggled on for what seemed like hours but had been in fact no more than thirty-five minutes. Which is a very, very long time in these circumstances.

With slumped shoulders and totally disgruntled with myself, and, I have to admit, with the agent, I made my way back to the office. Miss Heemstra took one look at me and shook her head. "That bad, eh?"

"That bad and worse, Miss Heemstra. He started out by dictating to me in French! For goodness sake, how can he expect a seventeen-year-old girl not only to speak French but take it in dictation?"

Miss Heemstra (trying to hide a smile) calmed me down and asked me to read to her what I'd gotten. I did, and with her help I even managed to type the whole letter.

I brought the letter back later for the agent's signature. He looked it over, beamed at me again, and said, "Excellent. I did write a good letter!"

I almost choked. He did? It was Miss Heemstra who had known the subject and had changed the letter until it was 'a good letter'. Later, I managed to get up the courage to tell the agent that he would do better to write down a letter in French, so that there would be no more problems with dictating to me. As it turned out, I could just write down in longhand all the letters in Dutch that he dictated, as he was slow and changed his mind often.

As time went on, I even learned to type letters dictated in Turkish (no, no, not by him!) even though I did not understand much of what I wrote!

CHAPTER THIRTY-SIX

This is about our social life and getting to know Mr. Lavroff.

There was a lot of that. Of social events, I mean. One of the first events my parents were invited to was a bridge evening at Engineer Lavroff's place for four tables. I was allowed to come along to watch and help serve the coffee and other drinks. I had watched my parents many times when they played and they had tried to teach me the rudiments of the game. I had never played myself yet but was interested to learn it.

I was quite self-conscious about the way I looked. I was five-foot six-inches and still chubby; there was no denying that. At seventeen that is not a nice thing to be either. On the other hand, I was quite anxious to meet that Mr. Lavroff again. For some inexplicable reason I wanted to hear him talk again. So, guess which table I chose to sit next to? Right, Mr. Lavroff's table. In between I helped prepare coffee and serve some snacks to the players. Mr. Lavroff seemed pleased to explain things to me now and then, but I realized that the game itself was of utmost interest to him. He was very concentrated. What amazed me was how well he anticipated the cards that people would play. It seemed as if he could remember every card that had been played. And when he managed to make a game that was almost unmakeable through sheer genius I was completely captivated.

All right, everyone. Hold your horses and your criticism. I was not thinking he might be husband material. How could I? He was married and thirty years older. I just thought he was a very fascinating person.

At that moment in the construction of the harbour of Zonguldak, we had approached the end. There were some small jobs still to be performed but the real job had been done already. The harbour was just about ready to be used. There was one big problem, though. The Turkish office in charge of supervising the construction for the government had been asking our agent how much weight the cargo quay wall could carry. He answered the number that was stated in the contract. Then they said, could we put more weight on it? Well, yes, some maybe. They, of course, had to try this out and put far more weight on the cargo quay wall than was specified in the contract.

Now we were in a lot of trouble. Our agent was not able to convince the Turks that the increased minimal movement of the quay wall was caused by them putting too much weight on it. They did not listen and said they would not pay us for building a 'defective' quay wall. Enter Mr. Lavroff. He had been hired by the company to untangle this mess.

So, who actually was Mr. Sergei Lavroff? He apparently was a Russian immigrant, who would receive Turkish nationality in a matter of months. Don't forget, this was 1953. He had left Russia in 1919, and only had the so-called Nansen pass to show his identity and no passport of any kind.

Serge Lavroff managed somehow to find a way to get an education, go to university, learn six languages and become a civil engineer in Turkey by the time he was twenty-three years old. He was a very gifted man. He loved sports of any kind, and had often made money by teaching tennis, by collecting the bowling pins after every game (there were no automatic machines at that time), by digging ditches, or doing any kind of work that was offered. That was his story in a nutshell.

Back to our social life. Other couples gave farewell parties and left, and after a few weeks Mrs. Lavroff decided that it was time for her to go back to Istanbul where they owned a beautiful apartment. Her parents apparently lived there with her. Mr. Lavroff decided that he did not want to live in his rented house anymore, but would move into the guest suite with the other bachelors. They had a good cook (my mother had been asked again to supervise), so he would not have to worry about hiring a cook for himself or any other servants.

CHAPTER THIRTY-SEVEN

In which I have office problems and my dad threatens me.

Mr. Lavroff took the same route to the harbor office as the rest of the bachelors, but he had his own transport. When the Dutch agent left, he took over the office to be in charge of the rest of the harbour construction finals, and so we saw each other now every day. He offered to let me come in his car and I gladly agreed. My dad was not thrilled with this preferential treatment, but Mr. Lavroff was now his boss so it was hard to say anything. Besides, again, there was nothing to worry about. We just really got along very well. And we enjoyed talking with each other at all the parties.

My dad enjoyed his work, and I liked to work in the office and not only because I could see and speak to Mr. Lavroff now much more easily. I really enjoyed the work and became quite proficient at most elements of office work. There was one big negative, though. There was another secretary—a Turkish one—who doted on our employer. She thought he was a great boss and a very superior human being. I whole-heartedly agreed with her, but she did not accept that. She thought I was distracting him from the serious work he had to do.

She was right in that his dealings with the Turkish government officials were indeed very tricky at this time. I knew that, but I could not see that the few times Mr. Lavroff and I had a cup of Turkish coffee (*chock sheckerly, lutfen—with lots of sugar, please*) when I was in the office with him, would do much damage to his image. Besides, he was then usually dictating a letter to me for the Amsterdam office in Dutch or English anyway.

Nevertheless, she had it in for me. She would put the blame on me any time there was some problem. It was hard to deal with this. Even just seeing her enter the office would turn me into shivering jelly. After all, I was only just eighteen by now and had very little defense against the accusations of this spiteful woman; she was really good at covering her tracks. And she was very much needed for the correspondence between the government representatives and our office. And that is how things proceeded for a good while.

I should have known that things could not go on like this forever. My father was getting more and more antsy about me going to the office with Mr. Lavroff. Then, one day he said, "Daughter, we have to talk."

Oh, oh, here comes trouble, I thought.

"Don't you understand that it is not advisable to be seeing so much of Mr. Lavroff? People have started to speak to us about it already. They keep saying that I should discourage you as this man is your father's boss, he is thirty years older than you, and besides that, he is married!"

I felt the color drain from my face when he said that. "But Dad," I said, "there is nothing between us. We just seem to really hit it off, that's all."

My dad did not buy into this at all. "No matter what you think, I must absolutely forbid you to go to the office with him in his car. And I advise you not to be seen talking with him so much during social times. You have to stop this or I will."

"How will you stop this?" I was outraged. Why could he not trust his own daughter?

"If you don't stop seeing him so often, I shall be forced to send you back to Holland."

That hurt. They had been so happy to see me here and now this. They thought the situation was serious enough to send me back to Holland if I did not obey. What should I do? I felt so lost and bewildered at the fact that my liking our boss (my father's and mine) so much would be deemed such a crime.

Looking back across the years I can now identify with my parents. I would very probably have dealt with it more or less the same way. What good parent will allow their only daughter (or any daughter) to fall for a man who is married and is thirty years older? Would you?

There was no one else to talk to about this but Mr. Lavroff himself. The next morning, I went again with him in his car and on the way to the office I told him what my father had said. He was quiet for a while and then he said with a sigh, "Yes, of course. Your father is right. I should have thought of this long before. But it is a fact that it is too late for me; I already love you too much—yet, how could I ever marry you; you are so young!"

I stared into his face. "What did you say? Do you mean that you really love me?" My heart was racing. *Dare I tell him how I felt?* "I don't know what I feel. I just hate to be anywhere where you are not. I only feel comfortable when you are near. Do you think that is love? I have never loved anybody before, but I do want so much to be with you all the time."

He stopped the car and turned towards me. "Even if you really do love me, what can we do about this?" His voice sounded sad and discouraged. Then he drove on to the office.

I was ecstatic that he loved me but the whole situation really was so hopeless. After all, he *was* married and he *was* thirty years older—those were the facts. When he stopped the car in front of the office he said, "I am very happy that you think you love me too." His face was so tender as he looked at me. "Let me think about this for a while."

CHAPTER THIRTY-EIGHT

In which we seek a solution for the situation between Mr. Lavroff and myself.

Back in my office, I forced myself to concentrate on the work I had to do. Afterwards, I was not sure what to do. Should I go with everybody else on the bus or should I wait as usual for Mr. Lavroff? I decided to wait.

It took a while, but finally his door opened and he came out. "Let's go," he said. "We have a lot to talk about!" He started driving but did not take the usual route; he drove in the opposite direction.

"Where are we going?" I asked. "I better get home soon; my father will expect me to."

"It's all right," he said. "I talked to your dad about us and told him we needed some time to discuss the situation."

I did not know whether to be pleased or not. How could there be anything to be pleased about? The facts had not changed.

He drove us to a small, primitive place where you could get some cold drinks and sit outside. Then he told me that he had sent a message to my father during the day, to come to the office to have a talk. He said that at first it was very embarrassing, but my dad soon lost his initial reluctance and told him that he was very unhappy about us seeing so much of each other. Dad said, "How could you make her like you so much? You are married, you are almost thirty years older than she is, you are my boss, and you just went and turned her head. When it comes to you, she is completely unreasonable! I don't know how to deal with this. It is so wrong on so many levels!"

Of course, Serge (as I shall now call him) had to agree that my dad was right. "The point is, "said Serge, "I have never met any woman with whom I can be so at ease and whom I like as much as I like your daughter. In fact, I LOVE your daughter, Mr. Smidt. And now I dare to hope that she loves me too."

My dad stared at him. "What are you saying? You can't love her; you are married!"

"Unfortunately, I am. My marriage has not meant anything for a great number of years. We live apart most of the time. We hardly ever talk. It is not a marriage."

"That is your problem! That has no bearing on the case here. I want you to stop seeing so much of my daughter. If necessary, I will resign!"

"No, no, Mr. Smidt. You don't need to resign. I am going to ask my wife for a divorce. As soon as I am divorced, I would like to marry your daughter. That is, if you would be willing to give your consent!"

At these words my father's jaw sagged open. "You want to marry my daughter? How can you even contemplate this idea?! You are older than I am! This is ridiculous. You can't be serious."

"Yes, I know. It is a crazy idea. The future will decide how crazy or ridiculous this idea is. She may tire of this so-much-older man pretty soon. I just hope that her love will survive all the obstacles we shall be facing in the future. All I can say is that I deeply love your daughter and would like your consent to marry her once I am free."

It took a while, apparently, but in the end my father, albeit reluctantly, had to say yes, he would give his consent. However, not without insisting that Serge would not drive me to the office anymore, and that he should be much more circumspect about being seen together with me. He told Serge to think of my reputation and to be much more discreet.

Serge agreed. He was happy to have my dad's word that he would not object anymore once he was free to ask me to become his wife.

I listened to this story spellbound. And when Serge said he was going to divorce his wife to marry me, I cried in earnest. I was so happy to hear those words. There was a future for us. I could hardly believe it. Before we drove home, Serge finally kissed me as we had both secretly wanted for so long. It was everything I had hoped it would be and so much more. I was suddenly ashamed again that I was not a virgin anymore. The feelings I'd had back then were so different from what I was feeling now for this man.

CHAPTER THIRTY-NINE

In which my troubles really start and Serge gets desperate.

Now we had to adjust our lives again. I went to the office by bus with the others. Convention was satisfied. We still had the occasional Turkish coffee together in his office, but we were much more careful as to when to have it. We did manage to go out for a drive on the weekends, though, and those times were wonderful. Also, my mother would sometimes invite him to dinner with us, and I did appreciate that a lot. It gave us all a chance to get used to being together as a family.

Serge had written his wife and asked for a divorce. Now we were waiting for her answer. We got it, but not in the way we expected. Serge got a letter from the main office telling him that they had received a complaint from his wife about the fact that her husband was having a relationship with me. She insisted that my father should be dismissed promptly as "he and his family were disruptive influences on the production of the company."

This was a serious accusation. Something definitely would have to be done. Serge answered the main office that he had asked his wife for a divorce as he wanted to marry me. This was her way of trying to fight this decision. He explained that their marriage had been in name only for a great number of years and that she hardly ever lived with him.

The company was not keen on firing my dad, but they did suggest that I should leave until Serge could get his divorce. That way they could show that they had done their best to 'get rid of the cause of the problem'. This had to satisfy the lady.

It did satisfy the lady. She probably hoped that now everything could go back to normal. That is, normal for her. She miscalculated completely the reaction of her husband. That she could write such a letter to our main office really upset Serge. He told her that it did not change anything; he wanted to divorce her even more now. In the meantime, we made preparations for me to go to Holland. My parents took leave for several weeks and came with me to help me settle in somewhere. I eventually went back to Aunt Nel and Aunt Akke in Hilversum.

Aunt Nel, who was a widow and a pharmacist by profession, was quite shocked when she found out who my choice of husband was. It was the fact that he was almost thirty years older than I was that weighed very heavily against my choice. And then the fact that he had to divorce his wife in order to marry me was also looked at askance. I tried to explain my feelings and Serge's, but to no avail. Aunt Nel and her family remained very sceptical. I don't blame them; it was a crazy thing to do.

It had been September when I came to Holland. Serge had driven us all to Istanbul and planned to go talk to his wife in person—she lived in their beautiful apartment and had her parents living there with her. Incidentally, whenever Serge had some leave to come home from his work in the interior of Turkey, there had never been a room available for him. He always had to sleep on the couch in the den... I only found this out much later. Serge did not want to talk very much about his wife while we were getting to know each other, but he would sometimes talk about the kind of life they had lived. He said that she was a beautiful woman and very accomplished. She was well educated and could have been a concert pianist, had she wanted to. She was also a rather cold woman, as I had found myself during our little trip by boat from Istanbul to Zonguldak. He had married her because, during one of his little holidays, he had taken her out once. His Turkish friends told him that this was paramount to an offer of marriage, and he now had to marry her. He eventually did, but the marriage had never been a very happy one. She did not want to have any children and, at the time, Serge had agreed with her. He felt that, living in a foreign country without even having a passport, he should not have any children because he had nothing to offer them.

When Serge told me this, I was surprised. I said, "Serge, I was seventeen when we met and I am now only just eighteen years old. I shall want to have children. Will you mind that very much?" I could not imagine that he would not want to have children with me, but because he was so much older, I could not be sure of that.

He smiled at me warmly, "Of course I want to have children with you. I want a boy with blond hair and green eyes, just like you!" Each minute we managed to spend together we talked about the future and what we would do. It was a most exciting time, the weeks just before my departure.

CHAPTER FORTY

*In which everybody has an opinion
and I get beautiful clothes.*

There was no stopping us now from seeing each other as much as possible. People soon learned of our plans and on the whole took it rather well. I am sure, though, that the tongues were wagging furiously behind our backs. They were also quite prepared to play a game of wait and see. Today I am a lot more cynical than I was back then, and I do realize that they must have been thinking that Serge could well be their boss on future projects, which would make me the boss's wife. It was wiser not to condemn too harshly this strange relationship.

My parents were not so lucky, unfortunately. They told me later how everybody had condemned them for even allowing me to see Serge anymore. It is true that even until the last moment Mom and Dad hoped that I would forget him during the months I would have to spend in Holland. This did not happen. When it is real love between two people, giving up is not an option.

There was another reason why my parents finally had to agree to my really marrying Serge once he was free. During our years spent in the Japanese concentration camp, the food had been so inadequate that many children developed physical problems afterwards. In my case, my thyroid glands were too slow, causing me to become too chubby on practically anything. I also discovered later that my uterus had not grown as it should. Serge had given us all kinds of ideas about how to lose weight, and I had tried to follow his suggestions. He did not mind that I was not as slim as I wanted to be, but I wanted to be as beautiful for him (and myself) as possible. I did start to lose weight, to my delight, and by the time I had to leave for Holland I was already not that chubby anymore.

In Holland, my parents took me shopping for my trousseau. At least, that is what my mother called it, but I know that my father just was happy to see how attractive his daughter could look in her new slim dresses.

However, I kept on losing weight and during the third week of our stay in Holland my parents took me to a doctor to have me checked out. He could not find a physical cause for my losing so much weight. He then started to ask more personal questions. "Is there any reason why your daughter is particularly stressed at this time?"

They hesitated, looked at each other, and finally admitted, "Well, she is in love with a very unsuitable man, who is also married. His wife keeps refusing to accept his terms for a divorce. And we, as her parents, are distraught about the whole thing. The man is almost thirty years older than she is. We are extremely perturbed about this whole situation."

The doctor sighed, shook his head at me, and then said, "Well, Mr. and Mr. Smidt, all I can say is that if you want to keep your daughter reasonably healthy you better let her have this man and be happy about it. There is no way to foresee how far her condition would deteriorate if you don't at least give her that."

I could have kissed him at those words! Finally, somebody who was not against me. I so hoped my parents would listen to him. Fortunately, they did come to the conclusion that it was better to 'go with the flow' without too many complaints anymore. It was a heavy load off my shoulders. Today I can understand them so much better than I could back then. I, too, would fight tooth and nail to get my daughter to change her mind in a case such as ours. I just knew that I loved Serge and that I wanted to be with him for the rest of our lives.

This is the first letter I received from Serge when I arrived in Holland and it did strange things to my heart, which was already in such a turmoil at having to leave him. He wrote it while still in Ankara where he had to wait for the train to take him back to Zonguldak.

My dearest Darling,

Before leaving for the train I have just a few minutes left to write to you. I have been moving around since I left you this morning just like a machine. My brain working. Discussing, smiling, eating. Inside of me there is a complete emptiness— emptiness of an abandoned well. I see what you mean to me. I see how much I love you and how much I am used to you. You know that I am a man of duty, that work during working hours is sacred, but today many, many times I was on the point of quitting—of going somewhere where there is nobody. I miss you—I long for you, and I love you. I know you must be feeling just the same and I am also suffering because of that. Love is everything in the world, but how cruel can it be sometimes....

CHAPTER FORTY-ONE

This is all about Serge's future in the company.

Serge had been very busy with meetings with the Dutch owners and managers of the Royal Netherlands Harbour Works company (RNHW) in Amsterdam, who had been in charge of building the harbour in Zonguldak. Apparently, the Turkish government had adjudicated the construction of a very large harbor in the South of Turkey (Mersin) to our company. The international auction by underbidding had been held on 4 April, 1954 and the ground-breaking ceremony was held on 25 April the same year. The government inspection authority was to be in Mersin itself. While under construction, the first pier was to be put in use by 30 August, 1958 and the last one by 30 June, 1961. The construction of the complementary buildings and structures like administrative buildings, passenger lounges, warehouses, and roads followed, but most of those had nothing to do with our company anymore.

It would take about six years, and it was predicted that it would open up the so-called hinterland of Anatolia. Serge was asked to be the director in charge of the actual construction of the harbour. There would be a Dutch agent who was to be in charge of the administrative side. This was a beautiful offer, and Serge was very happy to accept this assignment. He had considered emigrating with me to the States, but when this offer came along it was just too good to turn down. Later, he was also put in charge of overseeing any other jobs in Turkey that our company was involved with. Two of those jobs were NATO airfields to be built in Eastern Turkey. They cost Serge (and also myself) lots of head-aches.

I have all the letters describing all those discussions and meetings with our company managers, as well as with the Turkish government. Every time Serge left, he would write me and tell me all that was going on. I treasured those letters and still do!

Just imagine, our company heard on April 4, 1954 that they had won the adjudication, but they had not known that the official ground-breaking ceremony was to be held a mere three weeks later! I won't bore you with the details or by what nerves and haste the entrance of all our transport trucks, bulldozers, cranes, etc. into the city of Mersin was organized. I just know that my poor Serge was in the meantime trying to get his wife to grant him a divorce... What that man must have been going through is not imaginable.

I have this one picture of the ground-breaking ceremony with President Celal Bayar in the middle of the crowds in the town of Mersin with Serge close by. It must have been quite a sight because it seems as if the entire city of Mersin and surroundings was present at this exciting event. There were speeches by many of the dignitaries, all followed by loud, approving clapping of the people. I think Serge must have been very happy that night to be able to put his head on his pillow and know that he had survived the opening ceremonies.

The sleepy little town of Mersin was to turn into a great big and lively city after the harbor was finished, Forty-six years after we left, I took a group of my class of Ancient Civilizations, twenty-one people, to Turkey for three weeks and we also went to Mersin. I was completely taken aback as I could not recognize anything. All I saw were high rise buildings, beautiful shops, gorgeous boulevards—it had become a great city with over a million people living there. They had a big university too, and our little village had disappeared to make place for grand hotels along the seashore. Oh, I still loved it, though. I wish I could have stayed there for a while, but that was not possible.

CHAPTER FORTY-TWO

*This is about brothers and sisters
and babies—lots of babies!*

My dad left for Turkey and my mother and I stayed behind to wait for Serge's news. I had travelled with my parents by car from Turkey to Holland as my mother wanted to visit some of her brothers and sisters en route. She had had eight brothers and sisters. One of the sisters had died when she was fifteen. Her name was Hilda; she was the twin of one of the brothers. I am named after her, as well as after my mother's youngest sister, Edith. I met Edith once or twice. She was a really nice woman, but it horrified me to learn how her life had developed.

She had married a young man who was terrible at making money, but they were in love and did not worry about anything. Now, I understand about being very much in love, but the only thing Uncle Fritz was good at was making babies. And that he did. Every year came another baby for my poor Aunt Edith. And not much money coming in. I cannot understand how they could live like that. *(I must admit that I am quite judgemental—I am trying not to be, truly, but it keeps sneaking up on me!)* Why didn't they think far enough ahead to prevent all those babies being born? There were methods available even in those days, but Edith and her husband continued in the same haphazard and lackadaisical way and after number nine they had twins. Those twins were both intellectually disabled... It was at that point in time that my parents and I visited them.

Even my mother could not believe her eyes when she saw her sister. All her beauty and loveliness were gone. She was now just slovenly, uncared for, heavy, and tired. And then all those children. I remember one beautiful child with dark curls. Her name was Birgitta. She was so beautiful and happily smiled at us, but her cloths were pitiful and she looked unkempt. The worst was to see the new twins. I still shudder at the memory. What a life. What a price to pay for love without money.

Am I wrong to see it this way? I blame myself for being so harsh about this situation, considering what I was planning to do with my own life. I am not Mother Teresa. She could look at poverty and illness and disaster and just push up her sleeves and set to work, bless her. But I had just turned nineteen and I was simply horrified. I know that wasn't nice, but how would you have taken it?

After we left, my poor mother cried her eyes out. "Oh, Edith, what have you done to yourself?" It took a long time for Mom to put it behind her. They left money behind, of course, but that would not begin to help this family. I must admit that every time someone calls me Edith, I cringe, remembering my aunt. Today all my mother's brothers and sisters have died, but I wonder quite often what happened to all those children of Aunt Edith and Uncle Fritz.

We also stopped in Carlsruhe to visit Aunt Ella and her son Manfred. This visit went a little better, although even here there were problems. I guess, after so many years apart, one night's stay is not enough to bridge the time. Then we went to Bochum where the oldest sister, Aunt Fitta, lived. Here was where we always went to celebrate Christmas when my parents and I were in Holland.

Aunt Fitta had once had hopes of becoming an opera singer. She had a beautiful voice and absolutely adored singing. When her mama died, Aunt Fitta had been a young wife and mother, who was very happy with her husband. My grandfather was totally left-handed in the household with nine children, and had little patience for everybody's problems. Chaos ensued.

Aunt Fitta realized that she was the only one who could save the situation. As her husband, Uncle Heinz, was as near a saint as is humanly possible, he agreed to move into the ancestral home to look after the entire family. He gave up his own house and privacy, and she gave up any thought of ever becoming an opera singer. They pushed up their sleeves, like Mother Teresa, and saved an entire family from disaster. Soon everybody was starting to smile again and music was once more heard in the house. Bless their hearts. Their two daughters, Mausi and Ingrid, were my favorites, even today.

I am sure they also had hard times during the war, but a lot of that was due to Opa Noelle. He was violently anti-Hitler, and he never hesitated to tell anyone who wanted or didn't want to hear. It was always my poor Uncle Heinz who had to get him out of jail, with all kinds of stories how his poor father-in-law was not quite right in the head, and that they should not take his words seriously—he just did not know what he was saying. I don't know how he managed it, but Opa Noelle still lived in his own house at the end of the war. And he was still proclaiming his dislike of Hitler; but now everybody agreed with him!

CHAPTER FORTY-THREE

*In which we exchange letters—
lots of letters and despair daily.*

With all that travelling, my letters to Serge took a long time to reach him. He wrote me a letter on October 3, 1954, in which he complained bitterly about not hearing from me all the time. He addressed the letter to "My green-eyed darling!" After getting the complaints out of the way, he wrote:

> *Darling, I love you. Today it is again a Sunday and I long for you. Please come quickly when you can. After tomorrow it will be four weeks since I saw you last—it is ages, ages since I saw you last. Darling, I love you so much that I cannot be reasonable. I know I shall see you very soon, but how desperate I often am. I am so, so afraid to lose you. Although I am sure that your loyalty is as strong as your love for me, I am worried.*

I kept all his letters and put them in a big box, which was put in corners here and there during the many moves I had to make through-out my life. Recently I moved into my "Forever Home" in Lake Country, BC and finally found the box with all the letters again. What a discovery! It was so wonderful to relive those days of yore when times seemed hard, but had been so promising.

Yes, Serge was worried I would forget about him. He thought that a girl still in her teens could not possibly really love him. But I did. Every day was a very long one if there was no letter from Serge. Then; when there was a letter it never gave me the news I wanted to hear. He kept increasing the amount of money he would give his wife. It still was "No, I will not divorce you!" Then he would tell her that she could keep the apartment in Istanbul. No, that was not enough either. All this took time—one letter, one plea after another and the answer was always "No!"

I was often desperate and would cry myself to sleep. "Will I never be able to be with Serge again?" I would wail. Those were hard days. Aunt Nel tried to divert my thoughts as well as she could and so did the rest of her family, but I had only one thought—when can I go back to Turkey and see Serge again?

November passed. Serge kept writing his wonderful letters and kept writing that he would soon have good news but nothing came. And then it was December and I was counting the minutes, not hours till I would finally hear that she had agreed to divorce Serge at last.

And then it came, still unexpected. There was a loud knock on the door and it was a telegram from Serge! It was December 11, 1954.

"WIFE ACCEPTING DIVORCE LOVE ENDLESS LOVE SERGE"

I was ecstatic, of course. I danced around the house, hugged and kissed everybody and nearly drove them all crazy with my excitement. I immediately wrote a long and passionate letter to Serge, telling him how happy I was. As the euphoric feelings ebbed a little and sanity returned to my mind, it finally dawned on me that this did not mean that I could go straight away back to Turkey. Now I would have to wait to hear that the divorce was finalized. Only then would I be allowed to come back to Turkey. It was a sobering thought. How long would it take? This was Turkey. Would it be difficult? Nobody knew. All I could do was wait...and wait again.

Then it was Christmas. Lights, candles, small presents, cards, we all tried to make it a good celebration, but I just clutched Serge's letters to me in despair. When, oh when, would I get the news I wanted to hear?

CHAPTER FORTY-FOUR

Buying a wedding dress and more...

My parents had changed their attitude towards Serge in those days as they saw how much he missed me and how hard he had tried to get his divorce through. They now frequently invited him to have dinner with them, because all he wanted was to talk about me and how happy he would be to see me again.

My parents had by now moved to Mersin as well, as my father had been asked to join the company there. Mersin was a small town of around 35,000 people (and that included the area around it). There was a market where we could buy our fresh vegetables and meat. *(I was not always sure it was really beef I bought—there were too many darn camels around).* There was a nice beach but it was mostly occupied by small make-shift 'restaurants' where the main dish was always shish kebab. My mom was an eternal optimist as she never failed to ask, when she came in, "Schnitzel war me?" (*Do you have schnitzel?*)

Inevitably, the answer would be, "Yok, shish kebab war!" (*No, but we have shish kebab.*) Being German my mom still loved her schnitzel more than anything. She did eventually manage to get used to shish kebab and many other delicious Turkish dishes.

My parents and all the other Dutch personnel that had arrived by now, had rented houses or apartments where they could find them. This was a temporary measure as we were going to build a whole village just outside of the boundaries of the harbour-to-be-built. Right on the beach. There would be about thirty-six houses, a school, a tennis court, a volleyball field, and a mess for the bachelors. There would be a fence around the whole village and there would a bekci (watchman) at the entrance. The houses were being imported and were prefabricated.

All that, Serge had been telling me in his letters. I couldn't wait to become a part of the whole set-up. Serge had also told me that he found out that the final decision by the judge concerning the divorce was going to take place on January 28. There was still no guarantee that this would really happen. The judge could get sick, a comet could strike, or anything else terrible (in our eyes) could still happen, but we were really hoping that the 28th would be the day that made Serge a free man. He told me that I would have to contact Head Office in Amsterdam to arrange for my trip back to Turkey as soon as the divorce was finalized.

There were still a few weeks in January to get through, and I used those days to buy a bit of an outfit for our new house. Bed linen, tablecloths, kitchen linen; it was very exciting to be able to do that. Naturally, the most important item was my wedding dress. I had decided that I would buy something which I could also wear afterwards. I felt that Serge would not want me to do the whole white-wedding-dress-to-the-floor thing as he was so much older than I was and had had that kind of a wedding already. I thought he would appreciate the wedding to be a bit low key.

Well, I was wrong as wrong can be! Which I only discovered afterwards. I had managed to find a nice white dress with a soft mauve upper part, which would be hidden by a little jacket for the wedding. I bought nice shoes, nice undies, nightgowns, a dressing gown, summer dresses, stockings—lots of stockings. Goodness, how I hated to wear stockings. At least in Mersin it would be too hot for stockings during most of the year.

About the wedding itself I did not dare to think too much; it might jinx it. All I was waiting for was the 28th of January. Beyond that day I did not dare to think.

CHAPTER FORTY-FIVE

I am going to Turkey—I am going to see my Serge again...

January in Hilversum, Holland. It was cold and dreary outside most days. I did my shopping and started packing all the new things in a big suitcase, bought for this occasion. I received Serge's letter from the 21st of January on the 27th. Serge wrote:

Today only 7 days remain till the 28th. Endless days and endless nights...

Darling, we shall soon be together; we shall be together again never to part. Every sacrifice, every suffering and pain serve to unite us, sanctify our love, our most precious love. I need you the way you need me and even more. Remember, I am only a man and what is a man without the woman he loves? He is nothing. You can make out of me what you want because I love you...

I got afraid when I read this. I fully understood the responsibility he put on my shoulders with those words. Now it weighed heavily upon me. Did I do right by him? Yes, I loved him, but really, I was immature. In all his letters he was so patient with my impatience to be with him again. I must have made his life much more difficult than necessary. Oh, to be able to go back in time to be the really supportive woman he needed me to be....

It was the last letter I would receive from him, because I got the long-awaited telegram with the words, "Divorce is final. Come!" The Main Office people were very supportive and three days later I was flying to Istanbul. The next day I took the train to Mersin via Ankara, hoping that nothing would interfere with my arrival. It of course did not exactly work the way I wanted it to because there was flooding in the area. The train could only come to Tarsus, which was about thirty minutes away from Mersin. My dad and Serge managed to get a car across all the flooding and pick me up from Tarsus. I ran into Serge's arms, tears of happiness flooding my eyes. I stretched out one hand to salute my dad, but continued to stay as close as possible to Serge.

Ah... the long wait was finally over.

We went to my parents' house and I hugged my mother. She had been wonderful to me. She stayed in Holland for months even though she longed to be home with my dad.

Serge and I made happy plans and changed them again while laughing and joking, and in general behaved as only two people in love can behave. Serge stayed as long as he dared, but then I almost fell asleep because it had been a very long two days of traveling to get there. We hugged each other tightly and kissed each other with deep satisfaction. "Tomorrow we decide our wedding day," said Serge. "I am tired of waiting for you."

It was decided that we should get married on the 20th of March, two days after his birthday. It would be on a Saturday. Serge wanted to invite all the Dutch personnel as well as a host of Turkish business connections. We would get married at City Hall and have a large reception afterwards at the local Tujar club.

I agreed with everything. I didn't really care how or where, as long as we could be married.

Serge managed to get a lift for us in a beautiful car through a Lebanese connection who would be heading home to Beirut anyway. We booked into a nice hotel in Beirut for a week, and now all we needed to do was have a little white jacket made for my dress (me) and get back to building the harbor (Serge).

We chose Beirut because it was at that time considered to be the Paris of the Middle East.

Actually, Beirut already existed around 1500 BC. It got better known later when it became a Roman colony in 14 BC, and that is when the famous temples of Baalbek were created. I have seen depictions of what it probably looked like at the time—it must have been a glorious sight. Unfortunately, it is also an area where earthquakes happen rather frequently, and in 550 C.E. it was almost completely destroyed by the earthquakes themselves as well as by the resulting tidal waves.

It had been the territory of the old Phoenicians—those world travelers, but when the Eastern Roman Empire collapsed in 1453 AD due to their defeat by the Ottoman Turks, the entire Phoenician coastline soon became part of the Ottoman Empire. The Muslim conquerors rebuilt the Baalbek temples as well as they could, but it was no comparison to the original structures. After WWI the whole area was occupied by the Allied Forces and Baalbek fell under the mandate of the French from 1920-1943. After that they were granted independence. Many people in Beirut still speak French fluently.

CHAPTER FORTY-SIX

In which I get married but don't want to say, "I do."

We are getting married.

I got to know some of the newly-arrived Dutch people, and saw again some that I'd known already in Zonguldak and Golcuk when I was there with my parents. It seemed to be a little awkward for them as they didn't really know what to call me. Most of them knew me as John and Hetty's daughter, Edie. Now, I was going to marry one of the bosses. What should their attitude be? I worried about it as I did not want to cause Serge any difficulties.

The wedding day arrived and I got ready. I had washed my hair sparkling clean (I wore it short) and put a white ribbon around it. My make-up consisted of a little pink lipstick and that was it. I felt beautiful and loved by my parents and now by my wonderful husband-to-be; I was so excited and so happy.

The wedding ceremony itself was a blur as I did not understand a single word—it was in Turkish. The hall was beautifully decorated by flowers, especially irises. At a certain moment the man conducting the ceremony looked at me and said something. I thought, *Oh, he must want me to say "yes,"* so I said "Ewet" (*yes in Turkish*). The whole congregation started to laugh. I blushed and looked at Serge. He was laughing too. No, the man had not asked me the big question yet but something entirely different.

We continued the talk. Well, the fellow across from me continued the talk. Then he looked at me again and said something. I pressed my lips together and stared back at him not saying a word. I heard the rustling behind me of people moving but I wasn't going to be caught twice. Someone would have to make it completely clear to me when to say it.

Someone did. Serge's elbow hit me in the side and he hissed, say, "Yes now!"

I took a deep breath, put my shoulders back and said "Ewet!" And I was married

At the wedding reception everybody congratulated us all over again. They all now called me Mrs. Lavroff and I was thrilled to bits. Every time I heard that name I was smiling from ear to ear. However, before we left on our honeymoon, I laughed and said to the Dutch personnel, "I love it when you call me by that name, but when we get back from our honeymoon you can get back to normal and call me Edie again!" I think it lessened the slightly uncomfortable feeling I had sensed around me, for when we said goodbye, their wishes for a happy honeymoon sounded warmer than before.

We drove to Adana, which is about an hour's drive away from Mersin. Someone was going to pick up our car from there. Serge and I were almost delirious with happiness, and even though the hotel was nothing very exciting, it did not matter to us. We were finally together, alone at last.

Early the next morning Serge's friend from Beirut came to pick us up. *Ah, you thought I was going to describe our first night together; forget it! All I can say is it was worth it!*

The trip to Beirut was not very nice. We had many stops on the way by police; I never did find out what that was all about but then, there was always some kind of turmoil going on in Beirut. There were many tribal wars (*and they are still going on today*), and this was the turbulent and ancient Middle East. The road was not that great in those days. It took over ten hours for us, while even today it will still take almost eight hours via the new main road. It is about 550 kms today and it was a lot more back then.

But nothing could stop us. We were happy and decided to go out to the Kit Kat club that night for dinner and dancing. When we entered our room at the hotel, we looked at each other when we saw the arrangement. It was a large room and there was a bed in each corner of the room. The beds were single beds. Well, what could these honeymooners do? We saw that the beds were large enough for two so that was no problem.

I decided to ruffle the bedclothes a bit on the second bed the next morning so the maids would not think we had slept in one bed. O, dear, I was naive! As if they cared what people did. The next night when we came back to the room only one bed was made ready for the night...

We took a quick shower and headed out for the Kit Kat club. It was a beautiful place and I was beaming. I was also looking forward to the dancing after dinner. It had been so long since Serge and I had danced together. He ordered a beautiful dinner and we were both hungry by now. We drank an aperitive and toasted each other. "Here's to a wonderful honeymoon!" Then we started to talk about moving into our own house when we got back. Everything was so nice and good...but suddenly everything went black in front of my eyes.

I came to in a small room with the waiter and the manager staring down at me while Serge was holding my hand. He was so worried. I tried to sit up but they all stopped me. "No, no, stay down for a bit."

Serge thought I had fainted because we had had a few hectic days and then the long trip on top of that. I also had not eaten very much. All of that probably caused the faint. I again tried to sit up and said, "But I feel fine now. Let's go have dinner."

But Serge would not hear of it. No, he would take me back to the hotel and make sure that I got a good rest. Tomorrow was another day. What could I do?

Serge had to pay for the entire dinner, and this still bothers me. What a waste. And it was going to be such a good dinner too. Now we went to bed hungry…I thought Serge would be really upset about all this. After all, it was his honeymoon too. But he never said a word.

CHAPTER FORTY-SEVEN

In which I learn about the ways of the super-wealthy and see the marvels of Baalbek.

The week flew by. We went out for dinner and dancing, and were even invited by Mr. and Mrs. Gus Catoni to a cocktail party at their house. Gus Catoni was the owner of one or more shipping lines and his house was spectacular. There was a wide staircase going up to the first floor and on each side of every second step there stood a servant in a dashing costume. In the entrance hall stood Mr. and Mrs. Catoni. They were charming to us and welcomed us to Beirut. I told her how much I admired the flower arrangements that were displayed all around us. She smiled and said, "Yes, I love them too. I had them flown in from Nice (France) this morning." Then she said, "Tomorrow we are going to fly to the States."

Wait a minute, I thought. *She flew in the flowers this morning?* Obviously for this cocktail party, but tomorrow she (they) were flying to the States? My provincial mind immediately jumped to the cost of 'flying in' a dozen or more huge flower arrangements from Nice. Can you imagine the cost of such a thing? Yes, even in 1955 it was something only extremely wealthy people could afford to do. Well, I guess the Catonis must have been really, really, almost outrageously wealthy. My one consoling thought was, *I hope they send all these beautiful arrangements to hospitals and other deserving institutes.*

This did not mean that I did not enjoy the party. Serge was inundated with questions about the future harbor we were going to build, as it was going to bring much more business to the whole area. I was wearing one of my beautiful new cocktail dresses and felt like a movie star. We met many very interesting people who had a lot to say for themselves. I also received many compliments, which I tried to receive modestly (*though with great joy as I never had received many compliments before*), but which Serge did not like at all. There was no danger there as I only had eyes for my beloved husband.

One of the bank directors we met told us not to miss seeing Baalbek, one of the famous archeological sites in the Lebanon. His wife volunteered to take us there. I was so happy to see it, but I did not then realize how significant the site was. I knew Serge was interested in history; we had talked often about his coin collection with coins of the great Roman emperors and their stories. But now I know that seeing the ancient ruins of the temples and the incredible pillars in Baalbek must have been the start of my fascination with ancient history.

When I hear the word Baalbek, my eyes start to sparkle and I get inspired. I can talk and talk about it at such length that they have to tell me to shut up! You see, there are pillars that are so heavy to lift that we would have great difficulty lifting them today. So, tell me, how on earth did they lift these pillars up and transport them thousands of years ago? Oh, oh, I just heard someone say, "Okay, Edie, shut up!" Too bad. I was just going to explain...

Serge and I with our hostess and a guide I in Baalbek in front of the temple of Bacchus.

CHAPTER FORTY-EIGHT

We move into our own home and on the first day I miss something very important.

Going home was exciting too. This was my very first home with Serge. Once our prefab village was built, we would move there, but for now this was it. I had a Turkish woman come in to clean as was the custom there. My mother had prepared a nice dinner for us when we got to Mersin and we talked about all the things we had done and seen. Then we left. Together. And this was the first time I could go with Serge away from my old home. It felt so special.

The next day, Serge went to work and I unpacked our suitcases and roamed around my new domain. My own place, how wonderful. The first hours went by quickly as I moved things around to make it more mine. Then I sorted through all the books we had there and read a little. I went for a short visit to see my mother and that was fun. Home again I roamed around some more and wondered what other women did with their time. It seemed quite boring to me to be by myself with nothing to do. I looked at the clock frequently. When could I expect Serge home?

At long last I heard the sound of the door opening and I flew into Serge's arms. "Oh, I am so happy to see you again. How was work? Are you happy to see me too?"

Serge laughed and kissed me, saying that yes, he was happy to see me too, and he proved it by kissing me long and hard. I danced around the house saying how much I loved having a home with him and everything was wonderful. Then Serge said, "And, my darling wife, what are we having for dinner?"

Dinner? Oh. Right, that was what women did before their husbands got home—they made dinner. I blushed furiously and almost started to cry. "Oh, Serge, I forgot to cook dinner for us. Oh, how stupid of me. I am so sorry."

He started to laugh and said, "Well, that is a nice way to greet your husband of one week. Now we will have to starve." I was so ashamed of myself, but Serge quickly solved the problem. "Let's walk to one of those little places along the beach and get us some shish kebab. You can make me a beautiful meal tomorrow."

Cooking turned out to be more of a problem than I thought. My mom had never had much of a chance to teach me, so I had to consult a cookbook for everything. I really tried hard but chicken and I did not get along very well. One day I had done my best to make a nice chicken meal and Serge gamely chewed his way through the tough parts. Unfortunately, he tried too hard and with a crack he broke one of his teeth. It cost a lot of money to fix this tooth and I was apologizing for weeks afterwards.

Then I found a perfect solution. I asked the maid whether she could cook me a meal during her days at my place and teach me how to make those dishes. She was thrilled and she told all her friends, of whom many came to watch how she taught me. We all had lots of fun this way, I learned a bit more about cooking and Serge saved the rest of his teeth.

When we got back from our honeymoon, I had been quite disappointed to find out that I was not pregnant yet. We had talked so much and so long about having babies. And I remembered again the time when Serge had looked at me and said, "Darling, I want a boy as blond as you with your green eyes." I so wanted to get pregnant because I knew time would be a factor for Serge. At his age to start on a young family would not be easy, so the sooner we could have children the better it would be—for Serge and for the children.

CHAPTER FORTY-NINE

This is all about Serge and his family.

Who was Serge? It is high time for me to explain in more detail Serge's background and how he came to be in Turkey instead of living in Russia with his family. To start with, he was very proud to be a Russian even though his country was now communist. Russia was in his blood, and he would not hesitate to show his anger when anyone said anything denigrating about his country of birth. He could tolerate negative talk about the communist regime, but it really hurt him to have to listen to those attacking his country.

He made me promise that I would teach our children and grandchildren about his Russian origin, and how proud they could be of their heritage. Serge's grandfather had been a full general in the cavalry in the Imperial Russian Army, and Serge's father had been a lieutenant-colonel. Yes, the Lavroffs were royalists. Grandfather owned a large estate in Velikiye Luki, located on the meandering Lovat River and near the town of Pskov, where Serge was born. Serge had a brother, Arik, who was two years older than he was. The family often went to St. Petersburg where Grandfather owned an apartment where he liked to spend the winters. Serge and his family spent most of their winters in Pskoff itself. They always came to the estate

(*Raduzhnaya*) for the Christmas holidays. All the neighbours visited each other during this time. Everybody used horses and sleighs to get around.

Serge was born on March 18, 1906. When he was eight years old WWI started on the 28th of June, 1914 with the assassination of Archduke Franz Ferdinand in Sarajevo. A year later, Serge's nine's birthday fell during the spring holidays and so the family decided to go to Raduzhnaya again, as Serge was going to get a very special present. The family was asked to gather in one of the largest halls in the big house to start the celebrations. Serge was very excited. What would his present be this year?

Suddenly, there was a noise at the doors to the outside, and in walked an attendant, holding a magnificent horse by its halter. It had been Serge's greatest wish to have a big horse of his own, but he had not expected to see a horse walked into the house! This memory still lit up his eyes as he talked about it so many years later.

Serge had run away from school once, and Grandfather was told about it. He called Serge and said, "Sergey Vladimirovitch, I am very disappointed in you. I will not speak with you anymore, until I feel that you have repented enough. Just remember, Lavrovs don't run away; they stop to fight whatever battle there is!" Serge saw Grandfather every day at all mealtimes, but Grandfather did not salute him or say anything to him for days. Poor Serge was very upset and miserable. Finally, he broke down and sobbed to Grandfather, "Please, forgive me

Grandfather. Please, talk to me again. I truly am very repentant of having run away."

Grandfather was pleased, and thanked Serge for asking his forgiveness. Serge smiled through his tears and was so grateful that Grandfather was speaking to him again. The whole household had suffered along with them; everybody was relieved that this battle was over. They all knew it would not be the last one.

With the whole of Europe in an uproar, it was easy for the Bolshevik rebels in Russia to incite many people into a rebellion. In February 1917, the Russian revolution became a fact. As even a large contingent of the army went over to the side of the Bolshevik rebels, Tsar Nicholas II was forced to abdicate, ending the Romanov empirical rule in Russia, in June of 1917.

All these events had a great impact, even on small boys. Serge's father had to fight with the Imperial Russian Army and could only come home on very short leaves, as Russia was involved in WWI, as well as having to deal with their own rebellion. The situation became more and more dangerous as the Bolshevik rebels were gaining ground everywhere. The Lavrov family had, as usual, installed themselves on the estate as it was summer-time. They trusted their own people not to harm the family, but many rebels had infiltrated the countryside and incited the young men to "kill all the wealthy people."

Soon after the February 1917 start of the revolution, Grandfather decided to send for his son in order to get the family away from 'Raduzhnaya'. They were going to stay with their mother's sister in the south of Russia. She and her husband had two boys of about the same age as Serge and Arik, and she also had a daughter. Grandfather refused to leave. He said, "I have lived here all my life and my ancestors have lived on this property before me for a great number of years; I refuse to leave it!"

I first have to tell you another story about Grandfather. He had been married but had discovered that his wife had had an affair with his best friend. He was distraught. He challenged the man to a duel and killed him. Divorce in those days was unheard of, but not for Grandfather. He got special permission from the Tsar and divorced his wife. The Imperial Russian government banned her from Russia, and she was exiled; she apparently lived in Nice after that. *(Serge had discovered this by chance.)* It is hard to believe today, that a woman could be banned from her country because she had been unfaithful to her husband! Today we would run out of countries to send the women to; our own country would be flooded by other unfaithful wives. Oh, my, the thought of it makes me dizzy. I have a feeling Serge may have interpreted what he heard in the wrong way. At least, I certainly hope so. It was a fact, though, that she never returned to Russia and spent the rest of her life in Nice, France. Well, there are worse places to live in than the French Riviera!

Grandfather met another woman whom he loved deeply and he married her. They had a beautiful baby and were ecstatically happy. The boy, named Dimitri, died when he was eighteen.

They were desolate. Then Grandfather's wife got cancer. As do so many others today, he tried everything in his power to help her get well, but nothing worked. Then she died. Grandfather walked to her grave every single day for the rest of his life. I love the name Dimitri, but Serge would not let me call our son Dimitri. He said, "The name brings bad luck on the family."

When the rebels came to Raduzhnaya, Grandfather stood on the front steps and proudly asked them, "Why are you here?"

It was quiet for a moment, but then someone threw a stone and pandemonium broke out. Grandfather was shot to death.

CHAPTER FIFTY

More about Serge and "his" Russian Empire.

The people of Rus (as Russia was called) were originally Vikings from the land of Sweden who migrated to Eastern Europe in the 800s. They established a small kingdom under the rule of King Rurik. The Rurik Dynasty would rule the Rus for the next 900 years. This is the official version of the origin of a combined Russia.

Serge's version says that there was always fighting among the city states in the area around the 800s, and that was why they looked for a solution. No one wanted to accept any of the other city states, to be the one to unite them into one country. Finally, it was decided to invite three princes from Scandinavia to come to the area in order to try and unite the country. Their names were Sinius, Trouvor, and Rurik. Rurik settled in Kiev, Trouvor chose Pskoff, and Sinius established himself in Novgorod the Great. One of the members of the staff of Prince Trouvor is, according to Serge, his oldest ancestor. His name was Lavrius, and from there stems the name of Lavrov. *(Arik, Serge's brother, chose to write their name with two ffs at the end, after they left Russia, and Serge had to follow suit.)*

The Lavrovs lived in the Pskoff area for a very long time. These things must have been discussed at the dining table by members of the family, and Serge never forgot. I have tried to find out more about the Lavroff ancestry, but there I ran into a big problem. At the time of the revolution, most churches got ransacked and many of the registries were destroyed. There was no way to get any kind of information about the Lavroff ancestry. Anyway, not without spending a fortune.

The family stayed with the aunt and uncle for a few weeks or even months, but the situation became dangerous there as well. They all had to flee now. Serge's dad took them all over the country to small towns where he taught languages in local schools. Unfortunately, the Bolsheviks would soon discover their whereabouts, and so they would move again. This happened many times, but in the end, they could not sustain this way of life.

They found a ship in the Crimea that had some room for the boys, but the parents could not come with them. There simply was no more room. With a heavy heart the parents said goodbye to their boys. Serge was twelve at this time and his brother was fourteen. To help them cope, Father gave them many rubles, as well as a sword, but that was all he could do.

When the ship came to Istanbul, cholera had broken out on board. No-one was allowed to leave the ship. The boys tried to buy some things, but the money had become worthless overnight. Nobody wanted to buy rubles anymore. Serge and Arik were told that they could use their rubles as toilet paper!

Arik became ill and was sent to a hospital somewhere. Serge was taken to Egypt and lived in a tent-camp for refugees in the middle of the desert for two years. It was finally decided to send all the refugee boys to Greece to work in the fields, but Serge got lucky—the captain of the ship noticed the name Lavrov in the manifest. He called Serge and said, "I knew your grandfather, and I know he would want me to look after you. I will let you off in Istanbul. Go to the Russian Embassy there and they will help you further."

Serge was very grateful for this reprieve and asked the captain to also look out for his brother Arik, in case Arik was to be sent on the same kind of transport.

That is what happened. The embassy was non-existent anymore, officially, but they helped Serge to go to a Russian school. Later, he managed to go to the American University in Istanbul, boarding with another couple of Russian refugees and, by doing any kind of odd-job he could find, he could pay for the tuition fees. He became a civil engineer when he was twenty-three years old, and the rest is history.

CHAPTER FIFTY-ONE

Back to my own story!

A few months after we had moved into our first home, Serge announced that our prefab village was ready for us to move in. The first house on the beach was for the Dutch agent and his family, and we had the house next to it. There was a bit of a yard between us and the beach, but it was going to be difficult to grow any kind of grass on it as it was so close to the beautiful and sparkling but salty Mediterranean. We were going to try anyway and see what would happen.

The house was a bungalow with two bedrooms, a dining room, living room, kitchen, pantry, and one bathroom. I loved it. There were graveled lanes between all the houses and the gardener the company hired to beautify the whole little village planted lots of flowers everywhere. Serge had a small arch made at the entrance of our yard and planted sweet peas there, which bloomed profusely and smelled lovely. There were, I think, thirty-six houses, a school, the mess for the bachelors, a tennis-court, and a volley-ball field.

At the entrance to our village the bekci (*watchman*) reigned. I once asked him whether he had children. He said yes, he had children.

"How many?" I asked.

He put up his hand to show that he had five children. He looked very proud and I smiled.

"Are they boys or girls?"

No, all five were boys and he stuck out his chest with pride.

"Wonderful, but what a pity that you don't have any girls," I commiserated with him.

He frowned and mumbled, "I also have girls."

"Oh, good, how many girls do you have?"

Looking down he mumbled again, "I have five girls."

I was perplexed. He had told me he had five children and did not mention the girls at that time. Why was that?

Well, it seems that having boys is good because when they marry, their future wives bring in a dowry. The bigger the dowry the more popular the girl is. On the other hand, when a girl marries, she has to bring the dowry, so to have five girls is a very heavy load on a man's shoulders. No dowry, no marriage. Simple as that.

Initially, I had been very shocked because the bekci had at first denied the girls' existence, but later on I understood and sympathized with the poor bekci. I hoped that all his boys found girls with large dowries.

Serge and I settled into married life. It did not go without fights, though. Even though we were crazy about each other, we each had a temper. I remember one occasion where we had a real screaming fight. I was in the dining room and he was leaving through the door. I was so mad that I grabbed the first thing my hands found and threw it at him. Luckily, he just managed to close the door and the thing hit the door, denting it, and then fell on the floor. The floor consisted of tiles. The thing I had thrown had been a metal ash tray, very heavy. It broke the tile when it hit the floor.

I was completely shocked when I saw that. I had thrown such a heavy thing at my beloved Serge?! What was I thinking? It could have hit him. *Oh, my God, what have I done?* I rushed out to find Serge, flung my arms around him, and begged for his forgiveness, tears of remorse in my eyes. We hugged and kissed and he forgave me, but I had learned a good lesson. After that, any time I felt like throwing something at him I would check first to see how heavy the object was...

On one occasion, I think I was probably in the 'bad' period of the month, I had been nagging him about something. He said, "I don't want to talk about it anymore; it's a done deal and I am not changing my mind."

"Yes, but Serge, we could..." I did not stop the nagging; I was determined he should see it my way.

Suddenly he crooked his finger, and made me come to him. "Why, what are you going to do to me?" I asked suspiciously.

He said, "You'll see. Come here. Now."

I slowly came closer, then, suddenly, he grabbed me and put me over his knee. Then he proceeded to give me the treatment I probably deserved and smacked my bum repeatedly.

I gasped. "What are you doing!"

"Treating you like a child because you were behaving like a child."

Yes, he did. And, yes, I had deserved it. I started laughing because it actually was so funny. Then he started laughing too. He said tenderly, "Did I hurt you, darling?"

"Yes, my bum really hurts, but I guess I deserved it. I am so sorry for nagging, but I can't guarantee that I won't do it again."

Today, people are horrified to hear that a husband could smack his wife's rear end, but it used to be the right treatment for a naughty child. Smacks on the bum showed the child that this was his punishment for doing something wrong.

CHAPTER FIFTY-TWO

In which my mother shows the local ladies how to party.

My parents had a house close by, which was nice. We often went there to play bridge. I quickly learned the game and became reasonably good at it. We met local people through a reception we had been invited to. One couple became good friends very quickly. He was a Lebanese who came from Beirut. She was a beautiful German lady in her mid-thirties. She and my mother became very good friends both being German by birth. Yes, my mother. She was a very independent lady and did not hold with some of the local Turkish habits.

The first time we went to someone's place for a supper party, we were well-dressed and very interested to see how these people behaved at such an event. We came in and were warmly welcomed by the lady of the house in fluent French. That was fine; Serge was an expert in French. All I had to do was smile sweetly and mumble, "Comment allez-vous?"

As we walked in, we were led in a different direction. Serge and my dad had to go one way and the ladies were escorted to another room where there were only ladies. My mother and I proceeded to try to talk with several of the ladies. They mostly spoke Arabic, French, and Turkish. Hardly anyone knew any German or English. This caused a bit of a dilemma for my mother and myself. Later we learned that most of these people were very connected to the Lebanon through work or because they were Lebanese. And they were all Moslems, of course.

Serge and I. Some Turkish ladies had felt compelled to teach me a more sophisticated look.

Anyway, my mother decided that enough was enough. She squared her shoulders, stuck her chin in the air, and walked into the room where the men were talking with each other, smoking big cigars, and occasionally slapping each other on the shoulders. I looked back and saw the horrified faces of the other ladies. *Oh, oh, what is my mother up to now?* I thought uncomfortably. However, I felt I had to show solidarity so I followed her into the other room.

My father was happy to see my mother; she always did all the talking, and he called her to come over. He then introduced several of the men to us (I had closely followed her) and soon we were all happily discussing events with several of the men.

Serge joined us and introduced more men to us. We were starting to have a good time. Then I looked back to see what the other women would do. Ah ha, they were certainly curious, because they came slowly closer and closer until they too were getting involved with the men and merrily talking away.

Afterwards I managed to ask one of those ladies why we were separated to begin with. She started to laugh and said, "We have always done it this way. It was unheard of to join the men before. Don't forget, this is still a Moslem society. Moslems are very careful with their women. I think sometimes they wish we could be put back into a harem." And she laughed again. "Then your mother went there and you with her and we started to hear a lot of laughter. It all sounded much merrier than what we were engaged in, so we decided to see what would happen if we also joined in the fun."

I thanked her for her explanation and said that my mother just was not used to any kind of rule regarding men and women. In her eyes everyone was equal. The lady said yes, she could maybe understand that, but unfortunately it would take a little longer for people in this part of the world to realize that. All this was done in part French, part Turkish, with some Arab thrown in. I really liked this woman and said I hoped we would see each other again soon. After this event our social life really picked up. Everyone wanted to meet those crazy European women.

KISMET

The months slipped by, but every time I got my period I cried. Again nothing. It certainly was not for want of trying. Oh, why did I not get pregnant? Everyone assured us that it sometimes took time. "Just be patient and it will happen. Don't think about it. Then it will happen." How could I not think about it? I thought of hardly anything else these days. There were several young women in our Sahilkoy (Dune Village) and one after another they were having babies.

One lady who lived across from us had a lovely baby boy of one and a half when she got pregnant again. As she was feeding the new baby, her little boy disappeared. She called and called, put the baby down and ran outside to look for him, but it was too late. He had made it to the little pond in the mess area. He had drowned. It was terrible to watch her. She was desolate and could not stop crying. Someone had sent for her husband, and when she saw him she cried, "Jape, Jape, they say he is dead!" I shall never forget those words.

What do you say to someone at a moment like this? I was in my early twenties and just had no words; I did not know what to say or do, but in my heart, I cried with her. What an awful thing to happen in our little community. It took a while, but she was still very young. Her new baby was thriving and she got pregnant again. I was so happy for her, but I thought why can every other woman have a baby and why can't I?

CHAPTER FIFTY-THREE

In which I get very disappointed and someone shouts at Serge.

We had chosen one of the bachelors to be the mayor of our little village. We called it Duindorp in Dutch; Dune village in English. The Turkish equivalent was Sahil Koy, which meant Beach Village, in a free translation from the Dutch. Alexander, the new mayor, devised all kinds of events to keep the people from getting bored. Yes, how is it possible to be bored, living on the sensationally beautiful Mediterranean and having gorgeous weather most of the time, albeit a bit too warm in the summer. But yes, it is possible to get used to even the most beautiful place. So, Mayor Alexander arranged volleyball contests, special dance evenings, and also theatre productions.

I was invited to join the players and really enjoyed the roles I had. One of those plays was called *The Dangerous Corner* by J. B. Priestley. This was the plot:

Robert and Freda Caplan are entertaining guests at their country retreat. A chance remark by one of the guests ignites a series of devastating revelations, revealing a hitherto undiscovered tangle of clandestine relationships and dark secrets, the disclosures of which have tragic consequences. The play ends with time slipping back to the beginning of the evening and, the chance

KISMET

remark this time not being made, the secrets remain hidden and the "dangerous corner" is avoided.

I played the role of Olwen, a young guest at the house. In the third act I have to jump up and say, "Stop, stop, don't go on about it. Don't you understand? It is I who killed Robert!" It was a wonderful moment for an untried little actress like me, and I just loved it. The whole play went over quite well, and I was hooked. One of the other roles was played by "Betty," the wife of one of the divers we had working for us. We became quite good friends (*I thought*) and Serge and I sometimes played canasta with her and her husband.

A while later I found out that another play was being considered; Betty told me about it. She was asked to be in it. I wondered whether Mayor Alexander would ask me again, but I did not hear anything. I was very disappointed. When I asked Betty to tell me what the play was about, she became quite coy and said, "I am not allowed to talk about it."

I said, "But we both played in the last one and you know I am really interested."

No, she refused to discuss it with me. In fact, she seemed to enjoy thwarting my efforts to find out. She also seemed to be not at all sorry that I did not have a part in this play. I was hurt. I thought we had become quite good friends but apparently, I was very wrong.

Later, I thought it probably was a bit of what the Germans call *Schadenfreude*. It means malicious enjoyment derived *from* observing someone else's misfortune. She probably was not really malicious, but seeing the wife of one of the bosses being overlooked in favor of herself must have been quite satisfying. I tried not to mind too much but I did not forget the incident. And there were other incidents with other members of the Dutch personnel. Being such a young wife to one of the bosses must have been almost seen as an outrage to many of the older people. Some of them did not like the fact that Serge was a foreigner. The Turkish people doted on him, though, and that helped.

I was so proud of Serge for sailing through all these little, and sometimes big problems. He said, "I don't care what they think about me. I care how well they perform the job they are hired for." On one occasion he came home and told me that one of the men had come to him, shaking his fist and screaming nasty things at him. "You have no idea how to run this outfit, if you can't see that I need that crane very urgently right now. And there you go, sending it somewhere else. Don't you care at all that my work now is going to be delayed, you idiot?" And the man said many other things in his excitement.

I was outraged (I hope as a good wife should be) and said, "You should send him away immediately! Fire him! How can he say such things to you!"

And what did Serge do? HE LAUGHED!

I stared at him dumbfounded. "How can you laugh about this? Are you not mad at him?"

"No, of course not. This man is red-headed and comes from Friesland, just like your dad. This would explain, as I am often told, that he is extremely excitable, but he is also very honest and very proud of what he does. These are great qualities which I know how to appreciate. I just sat him down and explained exactly the reason why I had to take the big crane away from him. He soon simmered down, apologized for his outburst, and just said, 'But why did you not explain this to me first?'

"I said that I had been on the point of finding him to do just that, but that he had beaten me to it! We both laughed, and I promised him that he would get the crane back just as soon as the emergency had been dealt with."

CHAPTER FIFTY-FOUR

In which we go to Malatya and get a very unpleasant surprise in our bed.

Serge and I had been to the doctor to ask him what the reason could be that I was not getting pregnant. The doctor did some tests, some of which were very annoying for men, I was told, but Serge seemed to have all his soldiers in order. For me, the doctor sent me to Ankara, to the hospital, where they could do more intensive tests. The next time Serge had business in Ankara we went to the hospital, and they checked me out thoroughly. Then they told me that my uterus was rather small and that might be a reason the little fish could not get into the uterus so easily. I did not like the sound of that, but at least there was a good chance of ultimately getting pregnant. They suggested we just keep on trying. We were very prepared to do that. Serge kept telling me that we were so busy, there was no time to worry about this. I tried to laugh at this, but inside I was very upset.

We had been married about two years when Serge was asked to go to another one of the company's projects. This was an airfield to be built for NATO in Malatya. This town was about 660 km south-east from Ankara and about 500 km from Mersin. Our company was the silent partner in this project of another Dutch firm, which specialized in such works. They were, unfortunately, far behind in their building project and were losing a lot of money. Serge was asked to go there to see if he could do anything to improve the situation.

We had been told that a furnished house would be available for us and we could eat in the clubhouse if we wanted. We decided that would be the better way to go, so we set out happily on our journey. Today the roads are vastly improved compared to what they were back then, but we only just made it before dinner time. We were greeted by someone in charge and brought to our house where we unloaded what little luggage we had. After freshening up we made our way to the mess hall.

As we walked in, there were no friendly faces to greet us. Everyone looked morose and angry. Serge had warned me that the people might not be exactly pleased to see us there. They felt that they had done everything possible to get the work done and that there was no way it could be done any better. They thought Serge's arrival there was just an effort to show them that our company was much superior to theirs.

We both said good evening in a kind of general way and sat down where we were told to sit. The food was good and we enjoyed our dinner. We tried to start some sort of conversation, but it was clear that this was not welcome.

That night I made our bed and we were happy to go to sleep. It had been a long and weary day. We did not sleep well as we seemed to be scratching all night long. The next day we saw why. The white sheet I had put on the bed was covered with red spots. We had been bitten by numerous bedbugs. I was mad. How could they have put us into a house that had bedbugs?

Serge had told me the night before that he would go with one of the fellows to look over the site and all the works that had been done. I told him to go ahead and that I would try to find out what we could do about the bedbug problem. We had some breakfast at our own place and intended only to have the dinner at the mess hall.

I did not wait for Serge, but got dressed as quickly as I could and took off to find someone to complain to. I first went to the mess hall.

The cook was there and I told him what had happened. He said that no one in charge was around but that he was not surprised as the house had been inhabited by a simple Turkish family. Bedbugs probably were normal to them at that time, he said.

I vented my anger a little bit longer but was pleased that the cook did not seem so antagonistic anymore. I said we had to find a solution: being bitten all night long was not acceptable. He said DDT was the answer.

Then came the question of house help. Everyone seemed to have a young Turkish boy to help in the house. It was the norm at the time. I also asked the cook if he had a sewing machine hidden somewhere, but he laughed and said, no, but probably one of the women might have one. Our house had no curtains and Serge and I had not been married long enough not to want some real privacy, so I was determined to get some curtains.

I saw one of the women walk by and introduced myself to her. She was not very sympathetic. However, I did ask her if she knew anyone who could lend me a sewing machine to make some curtains. She started to shake her head before I could even formulate the question. No, no one would be able to lend me a sewing machine. And she walked away.

Ouch again. Bedbugs, no curtains, a hostile environment—we were going to have a really nice time here. At least Serge was there and he would always support me in everything, bless him. When he came home, he brought with him one of the men who wanted to explain to me the housing situation.

"You see," the man said, "when we heard that Mr. Lavroff was going to be joining us for a short while, we had no house available. Then the Turk who was living in the house with his family left, and so the house became available. Nobody thought to check out the condition of the house." For this he apologized profusely but that did not do much to comfort me.

"Just tell me what we can do, then, about those bedbugs," I said. "We can't live like this; they are horrible!" I remembered the camp years with all the bedbugs we had back then, and how it was impossible to get rid of them without any means to fight them.

I still shuddered in horror when I thought about it, and now we had them again.

"Buy lots of DDT and put that around the bed and around the sides," he suggested diligently. "And get a boy to help you wash the bed and everything else as well with a strong detergent."

I sighed. "I guess I will have to do that. And I need to buy material to make curtains for all these windows." Another sigh, but at least I knew now what I had to do. The cook had some DDT for me and I used that for the night. It helped a little but not enough. It would take a lot more DDT to get rid of these nasty critters.

CHAPTER FIFTY-FIVE

In which Serge shows them up and I get I get mad again.

Serge had walked over the site, had watched the trucks come and go, and had talked everything over with the men in charge, as he told me later. He had said, "The very first thing we are going to do is stop the trucks from going."

"What? Impossible! Every day we lose costs us capitals. We can't do that. No, no, that is just not right. Please, reconsider this decision!" they lamented, but Serge was adamant.

"What we have to do is fix the road first. This is the bottleneck that holds everything up. Every second truck gets stuck and prevents the next one from going or coming, and it takes far too much time to get those trucks running again. If we fix the road, there won't be any delays and we can produce a lot more work that way."

They finally reluctantly agreed and gave the order to start repairing the road first.

They lost two days of production, but the road was now easily navigable, and when the trucks started going again there were no hold-ups and many more trucks were producing much more of the work. This is one of the things Serge proposed to do that I could easily understand. There were other things too, but this one proved to be the turning point. Production rapidly improved, and the better things went, the more smiling faces we met in the mess hall.

We stayed there for two months. I duly bought lots and lots of DDT and some nice material for curtains. I did not find anyone who was ready to lend me her sewing machine, so I decided to do it all by hand. Yes, I can be very determined if I think something is the right thing to do. I started by making the bedroom windows; it was nice to really have some privacy, in spite of still having to fight the occasional bedbug. We were surrounded by DDT. I had put it everywhere I could think of in the house. It smelled terrible but it was worth it. The white sheet could even stay on for two days sometimes without a spot of blood on it. I made all the curtains in record time. Now we even had privacy in the living room—great.

Oh yes, I found a boy. This is how that came about. On day two, a boy came to my house and handed me a small piece of paper on which something was written. I squinted and read, "Could this viespeuk (*dirty ass*) be someone suitable for the Lavroffs?"

I gasped. How could he bring me this? As if a dirty ass was good enough for the Lavroffs? This was so insulting. This went beyond anything I was ready to take for Serge's sake.

I figuratively pushed up my sleeves and said, "Who gave you this?" By pointing and gesticulating and using the little bit of Turkish I knew, I made clear what I wanted to know. He turned around, went outside, and gestured to me to follow him. I did, and he went to one of the houses and pointed. I knocked on the door and the lady of the house opened it. I handed her over the slip of paper and said, "Did you write this?"

She looked at it and at my furious face...and then she started to laugh. She asked me to come in and said she was going to explain the "dirty ass" bit. The Dutch word was actually 'viespeuk' and has no literal translation into English.

Well, I thought, *dirty ass is bad enough.* We sat down while we left the boy on the stoop, after signaling him to wait.

First of all, the lady introduced herself, and then she said, "We all have boys here to help us. We would prefer the girls, but their parents won't let them work for us, so we have no choice. These boys are not the cleanest, needless to say, and they were soon called viespeuks [*plural*]." The actual meaning of the word started to fade, apparently, and everyone now spoke freely of the viespeuks. She forgot that I had no idea what these boys were called and she apologized for that. She said, "I knew that you would need someone, so when this boy came along, I thought of you. I showed it to my neighbor and she must have just sent the boy to you with the paper."

I felt slightly better upon hearing this, but still felt that it could have been handled a little better and with a bit more tact.

"No argument there," she said. "It certainly was not very tactful. But then," she reminded me, "we were all not very happy that your husband had to come here to show us how it should be done!"

"Well, that was hardly his and my fault," I said. "He was just asked to find out if he saw anything that could improve the situation. We did not really want to come here either. But, when the Main Office asks this from us, we can't say no, can we?"

That was the end of the viespeuk affair, but although my viespeuk did clean everything with the strong detergents I gave him, and he really tried hard to do what he was supposed to do, he was not beyond a little thieving. Not like a real criminal, but by using the opportunity when it presented itself. These people had so little and we seemed to have so much; they just did not think we would miss what they took. But more about that later.

CHAPTER FIFTY-SIX

*In which I lose my engagement ring
and Serge plays detective.*

While all this was going on, Serge had managed to improve the situation of the works considerably. They would not have a great loss for this work, and there would even be a little gain. This was more than the management had hoped for; so they were pleased, the people on site were now pleased, and we were pleased because now we could go back to Mersin. I gratefully prepared to pack our clothes and other things and got ready for our train journey to Mersin. We had been in Malatya for two months. Serge had once gone back to Mersin when there had been a problem, but had left the car there and taken the train back to Malatya.

I had all my jewelry with me, the luggage was in the car, and I said, "Let's go!" We got in the car that would take us to the train station, and suddenly I realized that I was not wearing my engagement ring. This was a ring with diamonds and sapphires and quite valuable.

Serge asked me some questions about where it could have been left. I told him that the only thing I'd given the boy, after we'd paid him off quite generously, was a little bag of chocolates. Serge told the driver to return and take us to the village where the boy lived. The driver knew where that was and we raced back.

The boy's family lived in a mud brick hut and Serge and I entered it. I noticed the folded-up sleeping mats against the walls and various pots and pans hanging on hooks on the wall. There was not much furniture to be found inside. I saw other children; older and younger than our boy. There was a father who was leaning against a wall and the mother was voluminously dressed in wide garments. She was seated on the floor, and she was wearing a head scarf.

They all looked at us with apprehension in their eyes. I was almost sorry for them but still, Serge was not going to let them get away with taking my beautiful ring. But, I asked myself, how on earth was he going to find where they might have hidden the ring? He did speak fluent Turkish, so asking questions was not a problem. He asked the mother what the boy had brought home from our place and she showed the little bag of chocolates in their colorful and shiny papers. It was on her lap. Serge took it from her hands, emptied the bag into his own hand, and there was my ring!

He returned the bag to her with a meaningful look and said, "Your boy has to be punished. He took this from us and now we take it back. It is precious to this lady [me]."

She protested volubly that the ring must have fallen in the bag by chance and that her boy was a good boy. Serge just shook his head, curtly said goodbye in Turkish, and we left.

I was clutching the ring which Serge had handed to me. I was very happy and relieved to have it back.

I had such mixed feelings. I was so happy to get the ring back and I was so impressed with the way Serge had discovered it but; on the other hand, these people had so little. I just could not blame them for trying to enrich themselves just a little bit. Serge turned to the driver, "And now get us to the train! With luck we will still make it." We just did, and looked forward to going home again.

Malatya was just a small town at the time, and having that big NATO airfield built there must have been a real boon to them. There were quite a few of those little mud-hut settlements on the outskirts of Malatya during those days. Today there are high rises and beautiful buildings galore and lovely avenues with expensive shops. I wonder whether there are still mud-hut settlements to be seen anywhere near Malatya? I sincerely hope not.

CHAPTER FIFTY-SEVEN

In which I meet my Gethsemane and survive.

Serge often had to go away for a few days to visit other works of our company to try to solve little or bigger problems. One of these places was Batman. Yes, the word Batman was coined already in 1939 in the West but the Turks did not know this. They had a river that meandered through the area, and the little town was named after this river; it was called the Batman river, a tributary of the Tigris. A batman was a Turkish unit which equaled 16.96 pounds. I know, boring. It used to be a little village of no importance but then, in 1940, oil was found in the area. Ah, now everyone was interested, including NATO. That is why they wanted another airfield built in the Batman area. It too ran into problems every once in a while, and that is where Serge came in.

It would take him two days to get there as even today it is almost 800 kms away from Mersin. The roads back then were a lot worse than now.

Serge did not mind too much, though. He was healthy and strong and took it in his stride, but he was always happy to come home again. He did not want to take me there, as the "hotel" along the way was not exactly luxurious. On the contrary; he told me that on one of his trips, the bathroom tap had leaked and it had driven him almost crazy to listen to it. He tried to fix it, but did not succeed.

He asked them to fix it. Same answer. The walls were very thin and he could also hear everything that was going on with the other people. "No," he said, "it is no place for you." The bed sagged, the bathtub had orange stains all over it, and there was no restaurant of any kind in or near this place. Then, at the site there was no place to stay either. Serge slept in one of the people's bedrooms while they had to sleep on the pull-out couch. He had protested that he could sleep on the couch, but they would not hear of it. I always missed him when he was away, but had to accept it.

We had gone to Europe on an extended leave, during one summer. We were by now quite desperate about how to get me pregnant. We had decided to have the artificial insemination done in Amsterdam with Serge's sperm. It was not a nice procedure, but we were ready for it. After that, we went on a tour of Europe by car. At our leisure. I kept hoping I would not get my period but when we came to a lovely hotel in Eastern France it happened.

I cried so hard that Serge could not take it anymore. He was upset too, but mostly for my sake. He yelled something at me and left the room, slamming the door behind him. He didn't come back for the longest time. I cried and cried until I finally ran out of liquid. Still no Serge. This was my Gethsemane, so to say. I realized that this desire for babies was beginning to ruin our lives.

When he came back, I was dry-eyed and even tried to smile. "Glad you are back, Serge. It is safe now; I am done crying."

He crushed me in his arms and almost cried himself now. "I can't stand to see you unhappy. I just want to do everything I can to make you happy. I really don't know what else we can do to make it happen."

I said, "Don't worry about this anymore. When you left like that, I felt so alone and miserable. I began to realize that all I need is to be with you. Everything else is a bonus, but you are the most important person in my life. Please, please, believe that."

He looked into my eyes and must have seen that I meant every word. He kissed me tenderly and hugged me even closer to him. "I will try to believe you, darling. Just smile, and I will be happy again."

The next few years I did try not to make too big of a deal of it every time I was late but then found out it was just a delay. Forgetting all about it was not possible, of course, but I tried not to make another drama of it.

CHAPTER FIFTY-EIGHT

In which we celebrate Laika's trip around the Earth again and the Christmas tree catches fire.

I had finally been asked again to join in the production of a sort of cabaret routine for the entertainment of the Dutch people in our Sahil Koy. I was very happy to collaborate in this idea, and proceeded to enjoy all the rehearsals. Serge and I had adopted a small dog in our second year in Sahil Koy. She was destined to be drowned and I could not stand the thought of it when I saw her. I took her home and hoped Serge would agree to keep her. He liked her as well, and so Spotty found a new and loving home with us.

We had already adopted a cat, which we named D.C. after Darn Cat in the Walt Disney movie called That Darn Cat. It took a few days but Spotty and D.C. ended up being great friends. I caught them once, defending our property against strange dogs. Spotty was barking fiercely and D.C. was hissing most impressively at the intruder. The strange dog must have been impressed, for he took off with a disdainful glance at Spotty; she was not much bigger than our D.C.

EDITH H. LAVROFF

**Spotty, D.C. (Darn Cat), and Rakker;
they were quite a three-some.**

One of our cabaret sketches depicted a space capsule that had just flown around Earth— one of the doors opened and Laika the dog would jump out, just like the real thing should have done, which had happened in November 1957. But what we did not know back then was that the Americans would be the first to land on the moon, with Neil Armstrong and Edwin 'Buzz' Aldrin becoming the first people to reach the moon when their Apollo 11 lunar lander, 'Eagle' touched down in the Sea of Tranquility on July 20, 1969. Remember, "One small step for Man but one giant leap for Mankind"? It was a heart-stopping event and I felt lucky to be able to witness it.

But the Russians had a first in that a living being—a dog, named Laika—was the first to orbit the earth in 1957 in the Sputnik II. The race for space was gathering speed back then, and it seems that the Russians might have been too hasty in sending out Sputnik II. There was a fault in the wiring, as is now known, which caused poor Laika to die of over-heating and stress within about seven hours after departure. However, she will always be known as the Russian heroine of space, who did orbit earth first.

Well, our 'space dog' duly jumped out of the capsule and caused great hilarity—it was our Spotty. She raced around and finally found my legs to lean against. I picked her up and said she was also a heroine. The whole show was a great success to the satisfaction of our entire group. These events were held in our school rooms. Yes, of course there had to be a school. Most of our people had children with them as the job was expected to last around six years. The walls in the schoolhouse could be moved around, which made it easy for large groups to gather.

All kinds of events were created to keep the people happy and occupied in their leisure hours. One day, not long before Christmas, Serge and I were asked if it was all right to have a New Year's Eve party at our house as we had a bit more space than most people, and they did not want to use the school. Everybody from our company who wanted to join us was welcome. We had also invited Ibrahim Miskawi and his wife Elizabeth, as well as our Danish friends, Bente and Paul Haestback. Somebody had brought us a tree that somewhat resembled a real Christmas tree, and I had put candles in the tree and happily decorated it.

The party went well. Everybody was happy and dancing and singing away. I looked around and sighed contentedly. It was times such as these that I realized how lucky I was. I was married to the man I loved passionately, my parents were near, we were living right on the Mediterranean in a nice little bungalow and had no money worries. My one big regret was of course still that I could not get pregnant. I pushed the thought away. I would not think about that tonight.

At midnight everybody hugged everybody else, and "Auld Lang Syne" was sung with abandon. Then the dance music started up again and people danced away with even more glee than before. I had lit the candles in the tree just before midnight but was standing right next to it with a bucket of water. Suddenly one couple waved a bit too much and swiped the tree. The candles fell over and the tree began to burn. For an instant all froze in horror. Then Serge grabbed the bucket and threw it over the burning tree. Others ran for more buckets and soon the fire was out. We all heaved a sigh of relief—that had been scary. They all helped to clean up the mess, but the mood to party more was gone; we had been sobered up in a hurry.

CHAPTER FIFTY-NINE

In which we have a more than happy Christmas dinner, but I get scolded for sending my maid Gulseiren home drunk.

Christmas 1958 it had been our turn to invite the Miskawis and the Haestbacks, as well as my parents over for the Christmas dinner. Over the years it had become a habit for us to spend this time together. All of us, except Ibrahim, who was a Moslem, wanted to celebrate Christmas, but even Ibrahim was fine with it. He said, "Any celebration is a good celebration." I had wanted to make it a real old-fashioned Christmas dinner with a real British Christmas pudding. I liked the idea of making it already weeks before the dinner party itself. I ignored the fact that I did not have the right ingredients and pots and pans, but decided to make do with what I had.

In order to steam the pudding, I boiled water in a large pot, then put the pudding pan in it so it could boil au-bain-marie. Unfortunately, this did not work. The pudding pan slid around and endangered the pudding. I scratched my head. What could I do to prevent this? Ah ha, I could put stones on the cover of the pudding pan to keep it in place and put some stones around it so it could not slide anymore. I tried it and it worked beautifully; I was so pleased. Every day I would put the pots on and I boiled religiously.

The only problem was that the stones tended to dance in the bubbling water, which made an awful racket. I was ready to stand it, but poor Serge got really annoyed. "How long do I have to listen to the rattling of those stones before you finish that damn pudding?" he shouted.

I figured that enough was enough so I stopped the process, hoping that the pudding would taste good anyway. I had a young girl, Gulseiren, to help me in the house. We got along really well. Her mother was very strict, though, and I had been told by her not give the girl anything like alcohol or other things forbidden in the Moslem world.

Christmas evening was there and they all came to our beautifully decorated house. The table looked lovely, and I was anticipating a warm and nice evening. Well, it became a little warmer and nicer than I had anticipated. At the end of the main dishes I came to the kitchen to bring in the famous pudding. As I did not have any real cognac or rum, I used Turkish cognac, hoping it would burn too.

I lit the Turkish cognac and started walking to the dining room, but the flames disappeared. *Oh well, I will just put a bit more on it,* I thought, and I poured another generous portion over the pudding. Oops, just before Gulseiren was ready to open the door to the dining room, the flames died again. I quickly sent the girl to get the bottle of cognac and poured more over the pudding. It burned, she opened the door, and everyone went, "Oh," and "Ah, how special." I smiled my happy smile and we dug in. "Anyone for some more pudding?" I asked.

"Yes, why not, it tastes really good," they said, and we had some more.

Gulseiren had gone back to the kitchen with the bottle of Turkish cognac. We finally rose to our feet but it was funny how difficult it was. We all stumbled and groped for support. Serge said, "I think we need more coffee!"

Gulseiren and I duly made more, and soon everyone was happily sipping away. They said, "What happened? Why do we feel so tipsy?"

I smiled apologetically and told them about the cognac disaster. Now they understood that they had not only had lots of pudding, but also lots of burned brandy! We all had more coffee and finally they felt ready to make the trip home. Serge and I rolled into bed with a happy sigh. He said sleepily, "I am so happy I won't have to listen to those darn stones rolling around in your pudding anymore; can we have a different dessert next time?"

The next day, Gulseiren's mother came to see me. She was very upset with me. "Why did you give my girl so much alcohol?" she said. "The girl came home drunk!"

I turned to look at Gulseiren and asked her, "Did you drink of the cognac last night?" I was quite surprised because she had never shown any inclination to have an alcoholic drink.

"No, no," she said. "All I had was the pudding."

Oh, oh. I forgot to tell her not to eat it...

I was no longer surprised that her mother was upset with me. I tried to explain to her mother as well as I could what had happened. Then I apologized profusely for not warning Gulseiren not to eat the pudding and said, "I will never make such a pudding again, so please forgive us both." Her mother finally relented and allowed Gulseiren to stay and help me again. We were both so relieved. Gulseiren dried her tears and I straightened my shoulders again, which had slumped when her mother attacked me so violently. And all was well again. But I never did make that pudding again!

CHAPTER SIXTY

In which we have a lovely time at Ibrahim and Elizabeth's place, but get an unpleasant surprise when we come home.

We had one more Christmas disaster, but this time it was not my fault. On the 24th of December, 1960, we had gone to Ibrahim and Elizabeth's place to celebrate Heiligen Abend (Holy Night) according to the German tradition. We exchanged gifts and watched their three children open their presents. We all had a lovely time. The next day it was our turn again to have the Christmas dinner at our place. I had been busy all week. No, no, don't worry. I was not making the Christmas pudding this time, just a nice mix of fruit and whipped cream. Nice and light and no cognac in sight. We all hugged and said, "Till tomorrow!"

Then Serge and I came home. We opened the door and were greeted by D.C. and Spotty, but what was that funny smell? We rushed in and I went straight to the kitchen. Oh, yak, what a disaster met my eyes! The whole kitchen was covered in black soot. I looked around and saw that the cooking plate I had put the big pot on with the soup bones was going full blast. I quickly turned it off. I had just put the pan on it, ready to start the next day; I had certainly not turned it on. What had happened?

Then I turned around and saw Serge's face. Oh, oh, now what? He said, "I am so sorry. Before we left home to-night I saw the pan sitting there and I thought why not start boiling it now? I will turn it off when we leave. But I obviously forgot to do that. I am so sorry."

Poor guy. I was not pleased with him, but he was so distraught at what he had done that I did not want to rub it in even more. I just said, "Next time, leave the cooking to me, okay?"

The entire house was sticky but the kitchen was impossible. All the soup bones had disintegrated as the water had disappeared after a while, and now the disintegrated bones sat on my walls, on the ceiling, on the floor, on the cupboards, in short on everything. You have no idea how black soot sticks to everything. It was truly awful.

I said, "Serge, let's go to bed. It is too late to do anything now. We will see what we can do tomorrow." He gratefully agreed. We tried to sleep, ignoring the smell of the soot and we also tried not to think about what the morrow would bring.

The next day I asked Serge to fetch Gulseiren for me and I went to see my parents to ask if my mom's maid could also help us. Then I started to sort out the kitchen. I put on my oldest clothes and tried just to concentrate on the one thing I was doing, without worrying about what to do about the dinner. Suddenly I heard voices, footsteps, many of them, come closer. The other ladies had heard from my mother about what had happened and all offered to help. I cried happy tears in gratitude and went about hugging them all. Between so many helping hands it was possible to clean the whole kitchen inside and out, as well as all the other surfaces that had received some of the soot in the rest of the house.

As soon as the cooking area was clean, I restarted to work on my dinner, without soup this time, but I did not think anyone would mind. I had no words enough with which to thank all the helping hands that day. But wasn't that truly a real Christian act of kindness? All these people also had their own Christmas dinners to worry about, but they still had found time to help us out. Instead of a terrible day it turned out to be one of the best we ever had.

When our guests started coming, the house smelled almost normal again. Serge and I were smiling, and when Paul and Bente came I got a really big surprise. Paul had just come back from Ankara and had brought me two dozen glorious red roses. There were no flower shops in Mersin at that time. It just wasn't something people were into. Me, a Dutch woman at heart, I missed getting flowers. When I saw Paul with his arms full of red roses, my heart missed a beat. It was such a glorious sight, especially after the hard times we had that day.

It seemed to make up for almost everything that had happened. Again, I thought how lucky I was to have friends like that and loved ones by my side. Serge saw my face and smiled. He knew what it meant to me. We had a wonderful time together and Serge and I told them everything that had happened that day. They were amazed that all had been cleaned up so fast. Yes, with many helping hands it had not even been that difficult.

1961 was just around the corner. Who knew what the new year would bring us? The harbour was close to being finished. We only had a year or so to stay there. Then it was on to new adventures.

CHAPTER SIXTY-ONE

In which Serge and I have a great time and I discuss the end of the Ottoman Empire.

First adventure of the year. We decided to go to Istanbul for a whole week for our local holiday. Serge wanted to show me an amphitheatre he had built. We intended to have nice dinners, go sight-seeing, and do a bit of night-clubbing while we were there. I also wanted to go to the Kapali Carshe (the Covered Bazaar) while we were there. It had lanes where copper works were being made and sold, others with carpets, carpets, carpets—we bought quite a few. Then there were lanes with leather works of all kinds, and each lane was a thrill to see. Serge and I both loved the lanes where antiquities were being sold. So exciting. We bought some old Turkish coffee cups, which were signed underneath with "Made in Constantinople."

In 1453 Constantinople was captured by the Ottoman Empire and made the Ottoman capital. When the Republic of Turkey was founded in 1923, the capital was moved to Ankara, and Constantinople was officially renamed Istanbul in 1930.

Serge had explained to me how Istanbul got its name. Apparently, the Greek occupants near Constantinople had always talked about going to the Big City. They said something like "Istimboli" and this became Istanbul over time.

(People both in the city and in the surrounding region referred to anything within its old walls as "εις την Πόλιν" (eis tin polin) or simply "in the city" and this phrase became "Istanbul" in Armenian and later in Turkish.)

Our coffee cups were made well before 1930 as they were made during the time that the sultan was still in power. He lost that power in 1922 when Mustafa Kemal Ataturk forced Sultan Mehmet VI (born 1861 in the beautiful Dolmabahce Palace) to abdicate. The sultan then was taken to Malta in exile and moved later to San Remo in Italy where he died in 1926.

The coffee cups we bought had beautiful brass holders which held the cups. The cups were scarred but we loved them. I still have them. When I look at them, I remember the turmoil the world was in at the time the cups were made.

The First World War had been a disaster for the Ottoman Empire. British and allied forces had conquered Baghdad, Damascus, and Jerusalem during the war and most of the Ottoman Empire then was divided amongst the European allies. At the San Remo conference of April 1920, the French were granted a mandate over Syria and the British were granted one over Palestine and Mesopotamia as these places were not considered ready to be independent.

On 10 August 1920, Sultan Mehmed's representatives signed the Treaty of Sèvres, *which recognized the mandates. Turkish nationalists rejected the settlement by the Sultan's four signatories. A new government, the* Turkish Grand National Assembly, *under the leadership of* Mustafa Kemal (Atatürk) *was formed on 23 April, 1920, in* Ankara *(then known as Angora). The new government denounced the rule of Mehmed VI and the Grand National Assembly of Turkey abolished the sultanate on 1 November 1922, and Mehmed VI was expelled from Constantinople.*

What an uneasy life he must have led. I was surprised that they had just forced him to abdicate. It would have been more in line if they had just killed him, like the Russians did with their Imperial family. It is definitely a plus in favor of the Turks.

I am sorry if I have bored many of you with my bits of history, but to me the history of the people of our world is such an amazing story that I can't help but talk about it. Maybe I can get you a bit more excited about it too!

When I went back to Turkey in 2006 with a group of people who had taken my class on Turkey's ancient history, the whole covered bazaar was a great disappointment to me. It was beautifully illuminated, and everything was much cleaner and neater than I remembered, but that old seductive and even a bit scary atmosphere was mostly gone. Here and there I still found some nooks and crannies where an old face half-covered with a large scarf, or a young woman heavily veiled would steal a look, not daring to expose themselves more. And I would think "Oh, not everything has changed…"

In the '50s everything had been darker, more mysterious, more exciting. I was of course very young at the time and it must have made a huge impression on me, for the first thing I wanted to see in Istanbul this time was the covered bazaar! When I went there with Serge it was of course much nicer as we managed to spend quite a bit of money there. This time, I only bought two small rugs (couldn't resist) and some other small items. I still love Turkey!

Serge and I had a great time and had lots of fun dancing the nights away, as they say. It was springtime in Istanbul— March 1961. The Mediterranean was bluer than ever and the water beckoned us to take a boat ride. I am sure there is no view more beautiful than the view of Istanbul off the Bosporus waters. Later, we danced at the rooftop Gar Casino nightclub. Serge whispered in my ear, "I still love you so much, my darling Poppy." Poppy was a name my dad used to call me, but Serge liked it too and often called me by that name. I smiled back at him, so happy. It was so romantic, dancing in Europe while looking at the lights of Asia on the other side of the Bosporus.

We also visited the majestic 6th-century Byzantine basilica, Hagia Sophia. It was built as a church but when the Turks took over, they turned the building into a mosque. There is one pillar which has a small hole in it. This was caused by the many women who had come here to ask for a special favor from their God. They would put their thumb into the hole and whisper their heart's desire, hoping their wishes would be granted. The Turkish women had done the same. Now the hole is quite deep and special measures have been taken to prevent the pillar from deteriorating too much.

When I was there, I could still put just my thumb into the hole, while whispering my greatest desire to the God of the Universe. It was March 1961. Oh, yes, I was no better than any of those other women who had stood there over the centuries, hoping for a miracle.

CHAPTER SIXTY-TWO

This is about bridge games and me being late.

We were pleased to be home again. Serge was itching to get back to work, and I went about having the house cleaned and gossiping with my mother. I told her all about the wonderful week we had, and she murmured all the right things. Spotty was happy to see us, of course, but my parents spoiled her very much. My dad had always wanted to have a dog but my mother always said, "No, I don't want a dog in the house." Poor dad. He took it because he adored my mother, but he consequently doted on little Spotty. My mother was not able to resist Spotty's cute ways and soon she was spoiling the dog even more than my dad already did. I remember one bridge evening of a few tables at my parents' place when the most delicious smells from the kitchen teased our noses. Someone said "Oh, Hetty, what are you making for us?"

And she replied, "It is not for you; it is for the dog!"

I had become quite a reasonable bridge player, but Serge could drive me wild with his observations when I had to play the deal. "I don't know what you are waiting for; it is so clear what you have to do!" he would say, when I hesitated a moment. Well, it wasn't always clear to me, and it would make me really mad. Yes, sparks often flew between us. But unfortunately, he was like that not only to me but also to his other partners. This did not go over well with them either, as one can imagine. They did not allow themselves to say much about this because he was their boss, after all, but it certainly did not give him any brownie points. I would tell him so later, but he would just laugh it off. "They are not as thin-skinned as you are, my darling." Hmmm. I was not so sure about that. He had an IQ of 157, but not everyone did. Mine was only 131; I had a good excuse! Well, actually 131 was not a bad I.Q. at all, but compared to Serge's 157 it was nothing, of course.

The weather was getting nice and warm already, hovering between twenty and twenty-three degrees Celsius. We did not have a real winter but we did need a little stove during the months of December, January, and February, for chilly days and evenings. In the summer it could sizzle in Mersin. Temperatures of over forty-five degrees have been recorded. But we always had the Mediterranean right on our doorstep, and this was really good in the hot summer days. By the way, I did not mention that I smoked. A lot. I had started while waiting with the other kids to hear whether we had passed our final oral high school exam. I was sure I would pass, but we were all nervous and wanting to know how good or how bad we had done. And this would be the last time we would see each other as classmates. After that, the real world was waiting for us. If I could have known what was in store for me, I would have puffed even harder on my first cigarette.

One evening we had been invited to a small cocktail party at somebody's house. I have a picture of myself standing there with a cigarette in my right hand and probably a glass of something in the other. In those days I drank only small sherries or champagne, if somebody bought it for me. Hard liquor was not for me. Yet. A few days after that party it dawned on me—I had not gotten my menstruation on time. I was always erratic in my monthly habits but I was certainly going to start counting the days. Three days went by and nothing happened. I tried not to get excited; it had happened so many times before. But how can you stop from getting excited about something that important? I hardly dared to breathe for fear that this would induce a period to show up.

Another three days went by and now I felt I had to tell Serge. I waited another day, then told him. "Serge, I don't know what is going on but I am ten days late."

His eyes widened and he stared at me. "Okay, that sounds interesting, but let's not get excited yet; we have been there before."

I nodded. *Okay, we will not get excited yet.* I closed my eyes. "Oh God, if this is another false alarm, then it is a cruel joke." I moved closer to Serge and he put his arms around me, holding me tight.

Four more days went by and still nothing. We decided to go to the doctor and ask him to do another frog test for us. We had done it before but it had come out negative. It was such distressing news to hear; sorry, but you are not pregnant.

I almost decided to wait it out because the thought of hearing that again was just intolerable. But we so wanted to know whether it was true or not. And then we went.

CHAPTER SIXTY-THREE

This is all about frog tests and waiting for the results.

The doctor was very sympathetic to our cause. Turkish men always want to have sons, so he knew how important it was for Serge to have a son. I hardly came into the equation but that didn't bother me. He let me give him a urine sample and told us to come back in two days.

The frog test had been developed in 1930 by a Doctor Hogben and was very reliable. They inject the woman's urine under the skin of the frog and then wait. If the woman is pregnant, then within five to twelve hours, the frog will produce a cluster of millimeter-sized black and white spheres. They did many tests, of course, during the trials but the frog test proved almost infallible. There was a saying in those days; the doctors may be wrong, but the frog never is.

Today there are so many easy ways to find out whether you are pregnant or not. I stopped following the procedures a long time ago. But in those days, this was the way it was done. Forty-eight excruciatingly long hours later, Serge and I got in the car and drove to the doctor's clinic. We were invited to sit down by the doctor and we sat. He did not speak any English but he knew that Serge's Turkish was excellent, so he looked at us and said, "Haberler iyi!"

Those are the most beautiful words in the Turkish language: "The news is good!" That means that you are pregnant!

We stared at him with wide-open eyes, not able to take the words in yet. Then Serge cleared his throat and asked, "Is it certain?"

"Ewet!" Yes, it was certain. To be on the safe side, the doctor suggested we take another test in a month's time. We nodded our agreement. Then the doctor proceeded to give Serge some more advice on how I should behave and what I should eat. He warned, "At the slightest sign of blood, just lie down at once and stay there". He would come around immediately.

We left, groping our way to the car. We got in and sat down. Serge did not start the car but turned around and looked at me. Then we finally began to smile, until I burst into tears. This time they were tears of joy. Could it really be true? Could I really be expecting Serge's child at long last? He finally started the car, and drove us home, going at a snail's pace and almost stopping at any possible little unevenness in the road. I laughed. "Serge, come on. You don't need to drive this slowly."

He gave a bit more gas and laughed sheepishly, "Yes, well, I have never driven my pregnant wife before."

We drove straight to my parents' house. They were waiting for us with anxious faces. My dad had stayed home to be there with my mother; they had suffered with us all those six long years. When they saw our smiling faces, they couldn't believe it and both of them started to cry—then all of us cried, hugging each other. I must say that this was probably one of the most special and happy days in all my life. Then Serge took me home, and went back to work, but his smiling face made everybody happy that day.

CHAPTER SIXTY-FOUR

In which we have another scare and I have to stay in bed because I am bleeding again....

I immediately stopped smoking, naturally. As if I would do anything to harm my baby—unthinkable. I now looked for baby books, baby clothes books, maternity clothes books, anything to do with babies. Was there anything else of interest in the entire world that could beat babies? Nothing, of course. The weeks went by in happy anticipation. When I was two months pregnant, the doctor said I should take another frog test. He was so afraid that I was not really pregnant because he saw how happy Serge and I were, that he forgot how reliable these frog tests were.

Then, one day it happened—I spotted blood. When I saw that I got ice cold with shock. *No, no, this could not be happening. No, no,* I cried inside. But I went straight to bed and tried not to move at all. The doctor came and took another urine sample with him. I tried not to feel too desperate because of Serge, but it was so hard. I hardly dared to go to the bathroom, but I had to eventually. No more blood had come. I pinched myself. Maybe all was not lost. I stayed in bed moving as little as possible, trying to think only positive and beautiful thoughts.

The next day there were no more blood spots and hope soared again. Serge went to see the doctor that day to find out what the new frog test said. By now I was again optimistic. I said "Serge, I must be pregnant. I just spotted a little but I didn't get my whole period. Don't worry so much."

He nodded, yes, yes, but he still looked worried.

When he came home from the doctor, I said with a smile, "Well, what did the frog test say?"

Serge hemmed and hawed and finally said, "Nothing. The frog died."

I was surprised. That was funny. Why would the frog die from a bit of urine? Then I decided to forget about it for now. I was still all right. I hadn't spotted more, and I was certain that I was pregnant.

Two days later I was violently ill in the morning. Serge could not believe it. "You really are pregnant," he said.

I laughed. "Were you not sure about that then?"

"No, I was not, because that second frog test did not work out. The frog did not die. It just did not give a positive."

Hmmm. I thought these tests were so reliable. Later, we found out that the frog might miss a pregnancy in very rare cases, but it would never show that the woman was pregnant if she was not. I was covered. Besides, every morning it was the same story. I was throwing up faithfully. I also could not stand the thought of meat. When I had to go shopping the driver would take me. He would have to order the meat because I could not get close to it without wanting to throw up. I was also getting tight in my panties, and I was looking forward to wearing maternity clothes.

Those were happy days. I was spoiled by everyone and my wonderful Gulseiren spoiled me most of all. I loved peaches and she would prepare me a whole plate full of peaches every morning, which I would consume in between the bouts of sickness. My cousin Ingrid from Germany came for a visit, together with her friend, Gely. I was still forced to stay in bed at the time. The doctor suggested I stay there until I was a good three-months pregnant. I acquiesced readily, but it was hard to see Ingrid and Gely having so much fun, going everywhere with Serge. I berated myself for being so silly, but I guess I was jealous—I wanted to be there, as well. I was finally pregnant but I could still be jealous of the others having fun without me, I ask you! I guess this must be because I do like to be the center of attention. It must be because I am a Leo. At least, that is my excuse.

At three months I started to have days where I was not sick in the morning and soon I was feeling fine again. Now, all we had to do was wait. I tried to walk as much as I could, did not smoke or drink, and I ate as healthily as I could. I often put on some light dance music and danced along to the beat of the music. Serge was very protective of me, which amused me no end. Such happy days. The summer months got warmer and warmer and walking had to be kept to the early morning hours or after the sun went down.

We would sit outside on our little patio, facing the sea, with a fan blasting some cooler air at us. There was not even a hint of rain. September came, but still no rain. The heat was overwhelming and I cradled my growing belly, wishing to feel the rain drops in my face. It was October before the first rain fell. I was outside with outstretched arms, my face lifted up to the sky, catching every rain drop I could. What a blessing. Not long now. We were both so impatient to see our baby. It was a boy, I knew it. I had a cradle covered in blue satin—there just was no doubt.

CHAPTER SIXTY-FIVE

In which we prepare for the birth, I almost leave Serge, and the roads get flooded.

To while away the hours, I would play solitaire at my desk. Would my baby be early? If the game came out, he would be early, but I had to play three games. It helped to pass the time. Isn't it funny how time flies when you are enjoying yourself, and how slow the hours pass when you are waiting? The 5th of December came along, which is the day the Dutch celebrate St. Nicolas' birthday. There was a celebration in the school for all the little children. My dad played St. Nicolas. Serge had allowed one of the tugboats to bring St. Nicolas to the shore, and all the children were beside themselves with excitement.

I was so heavy, I waddled instead of walked to the quay wall to see the arrival of St. Nicolas. I was still hoping my baby would announce himself today. No such luck. More solitaire games were played. *Is it going to be today?* The rest of the world had ceased to be of any significance whatsoever. The weather had been cloudy and rain threatened. This was all right, as long as we were not flooded as had happened sometimes.

Friday, the 8th of December, we were going to go to my parents' place for dinner and a game of bridge. We had found another lady, the wife of one of our bookkeepers who was a nurse by profession, ready to help me when the time came. She lived next door to my parents, so that eased my mind somewhat. Getting so close to the birth was very exciting, but also scary. Whatever the books said about giving birth, they all agreed it was not going to be painless.

What would my baby's birth be like? I managed to eat a little bit, but the Braxton Hicks contractions were bugging me now. It was hard to tell the difference between the real thing and these ones. They had been coming on for days now, so I knew the birth could not be far off. I sat down to play bridge. I was playing with Serge this time, but I told him to be nice to me and not to try and scold me for anything I might do wrong in his eyes. I was not prepared to be patient with him or anybody else. It took all my energy to just move around and think. He promised to be good.

Well, he may have tried to be 'good', but he didn't succeed. Even my mother got nervous about his remarks and said gently, "Serge, don't provoke her. We don't know what she will do."

Yes, it seems I was terrorizing everybody. I did try not to get upset with Serge but somewhere along the game I could not take it anymore. I cried, "Serge, if I could get up, I would leave you right now, never to speak to you again!"

This woke him up to the reality of the situation; it was not the game that was important, it was his wife, who was about to give birth, who was. We managed to get through the evening, but I was sore all over and the Braxton Hicks contractions seemed to get stronger all the time. And now there was pain as well. I did not dare to go to sleep because I was afraid the baby would come while I was sleeping.

No matter how many books I had read, I was still an innocent about real childbirth. We managed to get through the night, but by now I was having regular contractions. Serge alerted Henny Bothoff, the lady who had promised to help me, and she came. She timed the contractions but they were still too far apart to mean much. Henny told me to go for walks as much as I could. So, either my dad or Serge would walk with me, holding me during the contractions. After each walk, they let me sit for a while, but they urged me to try and walk as often as I could handle.

This went on hour after hour after hour. The poor men were exhausted and so was I. I told them, "Enough walking for now. I want to lie down for a bit. I will need some energy for the birth itself, you know!" By three in the afternoon it started raining. That took care of the walks outside, because it was raining just too hard. Inside I did try to walk back and forth now and then but I was getting quite impatient. *When is this going to end? When is the baby going to make an appearance?*

Henny was getting quite worried, although she tried not to show it. She did ask to alert the doctor. He came and examined me. "You have dilated about six centimetres, he said, "so there is a lot more that has to happen." My water hadn't broken yet either. He did not want to do anything to induce it. "Let it happen naturally," he said.

We had considered going to Ankara for the birth, but all the other women had had their babies the natural way, so why not me? The doctor had agreed with this, as everything seemed to be in the right place. I kept thinking about the fact that my uterus was rather on the small side. Could this have something to do with the slow procedure of the birth? Later, we discovered that the baby's head just wasn't entering the birth canal; it remained too high.

We suffered through the evening. My parents went home to catch a few minutes of sleep. Serge also fell asleep on the other bed. Henny stayed by my side. She kept looking at my body to see if the baby had 'dropped down' yet. Every time I questioningly looked at her, she shook her head. No, not yet.

Then my dad came and took his place next to me. They still tried to have me walk now and then. By three o'clock on Saturday night I was exhausted because of having contractions, lack of sleep, and too much walking.

CHAPTER SIXTY-SIX

In which the baby finally makes an appearance, the doctor says it's a girl, and Henny Bothoff saves the day.

At last, something was happening. I had gone to the bathroom and felt liquid gushing down my legs. My water had broken at last. Now, it could not be long anymore, I thought. Another hour went by, then another hour. My contractions came faster but the head of the baby just would not go down. By six a.m. Henny said, "It is time to call the doctor; something is definitely wrong."

The doctor came, then said curtly, "Cesarean!" And to Serge, "Bring her to my clinic." Then he left to get everything ready in the operating room.

It was Sunday, December 10, 1961. They helped me up, put a warm winter coat around me as well as a blanket, and then they helped me out to the car. It was still pouring with rain. Water was gushing down the paved narrow streets, the ocean was growling, and the wind was howling. I hardly noticed the weather. I was too busy having heavy contractions that went nowhere.

We started driving, then I heard water slosh. Our driver was driving the car and Serge was next to me. They looked at each other and the driver said, "It is all flooded!"

"Get through it somehow!" Serge told him through tight lips. "We have to get to the clinic." Somehow, we managed to get the car through all the inundations of the roads. Someone up there must have helped us, because for the next few days the roads were completely impassable; my visitors had to rent a rowboat to come and see me!

My doctor had found another doctor to come and assist him, but Henny was allowed in the operating room as well. She said later that she was keeping an eagle eye on how much anesthesia I was given, just in case. She said she would have knocked it out of the doctor's hands if he had tried to give too much. She was wonderful to have by my side.

Now I have to use Henny's words to describe the operation. "You went under easily, fortunately, and the surgeon cut into you right away to get the baby out. Once the whole baby was out, which took about five minutes, he held it in front of him with its back towards him. Then he said, '"Too bad, it is a girl."

Henny coughed discreetly and said, "Please, turn the baby around, Doctor." He did, his eyes opened wide, and he began to smile. "Mashallah, it is a boy! I thought for sure it was a girl because it was so chubby!"

They both laughed, and then a Turkish nurse took the baby out of the doctor's hands to weigh it. He was crying lustily by now. "Your baby's weight is 8.8 lbs." Henny told me. "But I was still keeping an eye on you because now the doctor took out the afterbirth and cleaned you everywhere. I saw that you were going to be all right. Then I saw that the nurse was trying to give your baby a bath. It was very cold in the operating room, and I knew that this was not a good idea, so I ripped the baby out of her hands, swaddled it in a blanket and ran out of the room with it, the nurse screaming after me. I saw Serge walking back and forth. I ran up to him, thrust the baby into his arms and said, 'Congratulations, it's a boy!' and then I ran back into the operating room to check up on you, meanwhile explaining to the nurse that bathing a newborn in such temperatures could have killed it. She was truly amazing.

Now back to Serge. He had sworn that he would not touch the baby until it was a year old. He had no experience with babies at all, and it scared him no end to think he would have to hold it. Yet, here he was, holding his newborn son in his arms. He carefully walked back into the room where my parents were waiting, while devouring the baby with his eyes. "It's a boy," he said softly and smiled widely. "I have a son. And you are the grandparents of a baby boy. Look at him." Now my mother took the baby into her arms. Serge sighed with relief. "Oh, I was so scared holding him. He is so tiny." Then he ran back towards the operating room to find out how I was faring.

The room they had given us held three beds. One was for me, the second one for Serge, and the third one was for my mother. My dad had to find his own way home again. At least, this was the plan, but my mother had been so nervous about the whole situation that she was a complete wreck by now. She saw me installed in my bed, barely conscious, then she put the baby in my arms and said, "You have a beautiful baby boy, dearest girl. Feast your eyes!"

I did, sighing in gratitude and happiness as I looked over every inch of my son. Everything was in order, everything was where it was supposed to be. He had no hair to speak of, but I knew that would come in time. "Thank you, thank you, thank you", I murmured, almost in a trance.

Henny had cleaned the baby and checked him out herself. Then she had dressed him in diapers and sleeping gear. I said, "Now I can sleep. I am so tired. Oh wait, when can I feed him?" Henny, who had also come into the room, said that I could feed him the next morning. She would be back to help me. I smiled my thanks, then closed my eyes and fell asleep. I knew Serge would be staying with me during the night. Henny had put the baby in his baby carriage, which we had brought with us (there was no good baby cradle in the clinic). Then my father decided to take my mother as well as Henny home. He promised to bring them back the next morning any which way, and indeed he would have to come by rowboat. Serge was going to stay with me.

Henny went with my parents but reassured me that she would help me with the feeding of the baby. I still don't know how they managed to make it back to Sahil Koy.

CHAPTER SIXTY-SEVEN

In which Serge has to change a diaper and the nurse gives me a dirty needle.

I woke up a little later and asked Serge to let me see the baby again. Serge said in a panic, "I don't dare to pick him up. I am scared to hold him."

I laughed. "No, you don't need to take him out; I just want to look at him in the pram.

A relieved Serge pushed the pram a little closer, and I leaned over a bit and saw my son again. I was very tired, but also so very, very happy. My baby was finally here. Serge sat next to me on the bed and smiled at the both of us tenderly. "We did it, my darling" he said, smiling at me. "We really do have a baby, and a son to boot. I am so proud of the both of you."

It is time we called him by his real name, don't you think? Serge wanted to give the baby a Russian name and we agreed on Michael, which was Michail in Russian. He would be, Russian-style, Michail Sergeyevitch Lavroff, said his proud daddy. In Russia, the habit was (and probably still is) to give a child only one name and then add to it "son of Sergey" or whatever the father's name was. When people meet for the first time in Russia, they will immediately ask for the father's name so they can call the other person, "Sergey Wladimirovitch" (son of Wladimir) as was the case with Serge. I would be Editha Ivanovna (daughter of Ivan—Johnny).

"By the way," said Serge, "I found a pair of old socks in my bed. I wonder how many generations of people have already slept in this bed!" He laughed softly. "But nothing can mar this experience; I would not exchange it for any other in my life. But what went before I knew the outcome—that I don't want to go through again! That was just too nerve-wracking." He had told me how scared he had been, having to hold his new-born baby son in his arms. I could well understand that; he was not used to kids of any age. Then he yawned and suggested we try and sleep some more. He would have to go to work the next day, poor guy. If he had known what his first job was going to be upon waking, he would not have been able to sleep a wink.

Baby Michael slept peacefully for quite a while. Now and then he would half wake up and make some baby sounds but soon he would be asleep again. I slept fitfully, listening in between for sounds from the pram. Around 5.30 a.m. the baby started to make more determined noises. Soon Serge woke up too. "What? What?" he said, alarmed.

I laughed softly. "I guess he needs a new diaper. You will have to change him, Serge."

He cringed. "No, no, not me. I will call someone. You can sit up and do it." He quickly left the room, then came back. "I don't see anyone."

"Oh, come on Serge. We have been practicing at home; you can do it. I will help you. Just put him next to me."

He carefully lifted the crying baby into his arms, then looked at me. "Now what do I do?"

"Just put him on the bed and tell him his daddy will look after him."

Serge was too nervous to smile at this remark, but he did manage to put the baby next to me on the bed. Together we got rid of all the blankets he was wrapped in, but then came the diaper. Serge carefully undid the safety pins and gave them to me. By now, I was trying not to laugh too hard because the concentration on Serge's face was something to behold. "Now what do I do?"

"You open the diaper, then you clean his bum a bit. Then you take away the diaper."

Serge did what he had to do, but then he took only one of the baby's legs in his left hand and started to pull the diaper away. By now I was laughing out loud; Serge was not; he was sweating. I said, "Stop, Serge, you have to take both feet in your left hand because now his right leg is dragging through the poop!" He did as I had told him, then managed to get the whole diaper away. Following my suggestions, he cleaned the baby, more or less adequately, and even put on a new diaper. He was inordinately proud of himself, and he had reason to be. At his age, he had done a remarkable thing that few men would have done better.

Henny Bothoff came later and helped me to feed Baby Michael. Fortunately, no problems there. My mother had brought all kinds of other useful things as I would have to stay in the clinic for ten days, according to the doctor. I had a huge scar from my navel all the way down. Yes, I know, these days women are told to get up right away, and they can often go home after two or three days. Their scars are now horizontal and not vertical, which is much better, of course. It was quite a bit different back then.

We also had other problems. As the room was so cold, we used a small electric stove to bring some extra heat into the room. Their electricity was not adequate to take this all the time so someone would have to push the switch back every couple of hours. And then there was the hospital staff. They were very nice and accommodating but not very up-to-date in their methods.

We managed to get through one day in which there was only one incident that really shocked us all. The nurse came to give me a penicillin shot. She accidentally dropped the needle, then bent and picked it up off the floor and proceeded to try and give me the injection. I was lucky enough to have Henny Bothoff there. She screamed "Stop!"

The nurse looked at her in amazement. "Why do you not want me to give the injection?" she said.

"Because you cannot reuse the same needle you dropped on the floor," Henny said. "Please, get a new one."

"But it does not matter if the needle is not clean; this is penicillin," the nurse stated.

"It matters very much that it is not clean anymore," Henny explained. "Never ever do that again; it is very bad."

Shrugging her shoulders, the nurse went to get another needle. We were all shocked by her lack of knowledge regarding these things, but it was nothing compared to what the doctor himself did the next day.

CHAPTER SIXTY-EIGHT

In which a proud doctor shows us what he took out of his latest patient and I get a high fever.

My mother had given me the baby to nurse. She was fondly watching us both; a very proud and happy grandmother. She was in charge of changing his diapers. She had just given him a clean nappie and had wrapped him warmly in his blanket before giving him to me. Suddenly, the door was thrown open and the doctor appeared, holding a bowl with something very bloody in it. His white coat was covered in blood, but his face was triumphant: "Look," he called out. "I have just removed this from my patient's body and the man is still alive!"

My mother jumped to her feet and shouted, "Out, out! How dare you come in here like that when there is a newborn baby and a woman who was just operated on? Out!"

The doctor looked very disappointed at this reception. He had not understood what my mother was saying, but he knew the meaning of the pointing finger—out! When Serge came, we told him about it, and he went in search of the doctor to explain why we had been so upset. And also, to congratulate the doctor on removing whatever part of the body it was he had removed, while keeping the man alive. Serge knew how to deal with the Turks; he had lived long enough in Turkey to know. The doctor meant well, but was just not quite used to up-to-date matters. So, Serge did a bit of 'oiling': "Yes, they are so afraid of germs…"

On day four, I thought the milk was starting to really come in. Baby was drinking beautifully every three hours or so. I was happy when I had him with me, but the long bandage they had wrapped around my belly was beginning to bother me. The nurses had not done much more than to bring some food or tea, or to give me injections. I guess they thought that Henny Bothoff was going to do the rest, but Henny said, "No, it is their job to wash you and in general help you to get clean." So, we asked the nurse when she was going to remove the long, wide bandage around my abdomen. It had really helped me to get the size of my belly down, but I was ready to get cleaned up.

The nurse looked at me in surprise. "Why would you want me to remove this bandage and the pads; any new ones will only get dirty again."

We looked at each other in stunned disbelief. Then Henny Bothoff smiled— this was Mersin in southern Turkey in 1961 and not Amsterdam. We begged the nurse to indulge me and to get me a clean bandage and other necessary things for washing me. She finally shrugged her shoulders and disappeared, to come back a few minutes later with some warm water, as well as a new wide bandage and pads. When all the necessary was done, I felt clean again at long last.

On the fifth day, my fever really started up. I kept saying that it must be because the milk was coming in, but nobody listened. Henny stayed that evening, as well as my mom and dad, and Serge, of course. Any one of them would take a bed to sleep in for a while. There were two other beds anyway. My fever was going up and up, and I was not so much with it anymore. But the baby wanted milk every two or three hours. He had a good loud voice, which woke up everybody. Henny Bothoff would just turn me around a little and put the baby to drink, me being hot or not. Then baby would happily fall asleep again.

Around midnight, my dad said he would take Henny and my mother home. Serge knew the routine by now and was ready to stay. The fever, however, did not slow down. It stayed quite high. The doctor came early in the morning to check up on me and took Serge aside. Later, Serge told me that he wanted me to go home because he thought the clinic was killing me. Too many germs, too little electricity, too little knowledge in the whole team, he said. "Your wife will be better off at home where it is clean and she can build up her own routine. I will come and see her every other day for the first week."

On day six, Serge took his wife and son home.

How wonderful it was to be in my own surroundings again. I soon started to move around and the fever disappeared. Baby Michael was thriving, and we all adored him. Two weeks after baby's birth it was Christmas. There was a party at the school building and both Serge and I went. Serge had stationed a guard in front of the window of Baby Michael's room with the instruction to come to get one of us when he started crying.

And one of us went home every hour to check up on our baby. Those were happy days. The floods had receded and it was again possible to use a car. The new year beckoned with its new adventures. We had our longed-for baby, and the future looked bright with promise.

Serge and I with 10 day old Baby Michael.

CHAPTER SIXTY-NINE

The job is done, and we are ready to go to Holland.

Before our departure, Serge's brother, Arik, and his wife, Fahrida—a Christian Maronite Lebanese lady—paid us a visit to make the acquaintance of their brand-new nephew. In fact, Fahrida—who had wanted very much to have children of her own but never did—had given me a special ribbon that she had made. She had told me, before I finally got pregnant, that she had taken it to her church to be blessed, especially to help me to get pregnant. I had to wear it around my waist every time we had sex, Serge and I. She was so sincere and so loving that I promised her I would do exactly as she had told me. I was ready to try anything to get pregnant. I did wear the ribbon throughout after that, and when I did get pregnant I gave her the credit. She was so thrilled to hear this that she told everyone how it had worked for me.

When the baby was five months old, we were ready to go to Holland. Somebody else was left in charge to finish the remaining tasks. I had booked us some rooms in a private house somewhere in Amsterdam-South, and we were looking forward to spending some time there while searching for a flat of our own. Serge was going to be working on some new projects at the Main Office, but he did not know yet to what place he would be sent next.

**Arik, Fahrida, Serge, myself with baby Michael,
my dad, and my mom.**

We looked at a variety of apartments, and finally decided on a really beautiful one with two bedrooms, dining-living room, and kitchen on the second floor of a new apartment building in South Amsterdam. What spoke to me the most was that the baby's room had been decorated all over, even the ceiling, with beautiful wallpaper with pink and blue happy birds and flowers on them. It was such a lovely room for a small baby to stay in that we could not resist. We bought the place.

While we were in Holland, we would often take our Mikey to my parents' place in Vinkeveen, about half an hour away from Amsterdam and also from us. It was a whole new development—verdant cow pastures were turned into rows and rows of attractive homes and soon all the pastures were gone. My parents had taken the overland route to go back to Holland from Turkey, and had taken our little Spotty with them. D.C. was going to stay with our driver who really liked him.

My mother wanted to visit her family back in Germany, en route. My parents loved their new home and made friends with many of the neighboring families. One of those ladies was expecting a baby to be born in early December.

When Michael was two years old, he met that baby. She was in her play pen and Mikey tried to get at her toys inside the pen. She started to cry out at sighting him and we all rushed out to see what was going on. This first encounter turned into a strong and lasting friendship. Mikey bossed her around and she followed him slavishly for many years when we were in Holland. Her name was Janine van der Laaken; her father was a navigator for KLM. She always said that she was going to marry Michael when she grew up. When she was four years old, she had to go to the bathroom. I helped her and then she said, "Auntie Edie, who is going to clean my bum when Mikey and I are married?" She was one determined young lady!

We had decided that it would be nice to have a property with some land. We wanted to build a house on it. It had to be as close to Amsterdam as we could find because of Serge's work. We went and viewed some beautiful properties but the one would be too far away, the other would be too old, and again another one was nice but was not in a nice-enough area. Finally, we came upon a piece of land that was only two-thirds of an acre, but it was in a fantastic area and had a lovely forest right across from the property. It was also more than Serge was ready to spend.

I said, "Serge, this is absolutely perfect. We will never, ever find anything like this anywhere else."

"Yes, but.... the price. We really should not put that much money into just the land."

I told him that he should go ahead and try to find something else. I had seen what I thought was ideal but I would go with his decision. He did go out a couple of times, but one day he came home and said, "I have bought your acreage today!"

I jumped a mile in the air and hugged him over and over again. "You will not regret this decision. We will just have to be a little more careful not to spend too much on the house itself."

Serge came home one time, and said, "We have a new place to go to!"

I jumped up, all excited. "Where, where, are we going?"

"We are going to Aden. We have to build three oil-tanker island-jetties for the huge oil tankers that are too big to enter into the harbor itself. Actually, they are islands with a long quay wall on them, where the tankers can lay over."

"Oh, are you pleased with this new assignment?" I asked.

"Yes, very. It is a challenging job and I look forward to it. It will only take two years."

Serge was fifty-six now and still looked really good—certainly in my eyes. He adored his little son and Mikey adored him. "Now, tell me all about Aden, Serge." I said. "Oh, by the way, when are we leaving?"

"Early January 1963. I thought you might want to celebrate Christmas here with your parents. Am I right?."

Yes, of course he was right. I knew my parents would not be pleased to be separated from their little grandson, but my dad had always taught me that the job came before everything else, so he would understand. He was a military man; still a soldier at heart.

Aden lies on the southernmost point of Saudi Arabia and the Yemen. The British had come to Aden in 1839 to stop attacks by pirates against British shipping to India. They could now better control the entrance to the Red Sea. The British wanted to create protectorates along the Red Sea as a buffer against the Ottomans, who occupied the country of Yemen. In 1937 Aden became a Crown Colony. In 1962 the British Government announced that a permanent British garrison would be maintained in Aden, but in 1967 they were forced to withdraw from the colony due to a lot of unrest, caused by Arab nationalism as well as anti-colonialism.

CHAPTER SEVENTY

In which I have two servants but have to clean my own toilets and Serge's secretary, Patricia, goes camel-racing.

We arrived in Aden early January 1963. Baby Michael was now one-year-old. On his first birthday he had decided that milk was not to his liking anymore. I was used to give him a bottle around six in the morning, just to keep him occupied a little while longer while we stayed in bed. That morning he accepted the bottle, looked at it in disdain, then proceeded to throw the bottle away into the room. I was perplexed. "Don't you want your milky?" I asked. He refused the bottle again when I offered it to him a second time. *Okay*, I thought, *now what do we do?* I got him a cookie and left to complain to Serge.

Michael did not drink milk anymore until he was four years old, the little rascal. He remained very difficult about food, unfortunately.

During the trip by air he was very hard to handle as he tried to press any buttons he could find. He also tried to pat all the heads ahead of him, which was not really appreciated. To our despair, he did not go to sleep during the entire flight. I looked at Serge's tired eyes and I said, "Are you still happy to have a son?"

Immediately a huge smile came across his face. "You bet I am. Look at him! He is the best and most handsome little boy in the entire universe!" I fully agreed with him, of course.

We circled over the Aden airfield and were getting ready to come down when I looked over at Mikey: he was asleep at long last..."

Aden turned out to be a nice-enough place with large governmental buildings and many nice shops downtown. But the barren, rocky outcroppings right behind it gave it a feeling of desolation. There were very few trees, but there was one place on the outskirts of Aden that had been created as a park, with nice walkways, plants, and trees. We loved going there. For the rest, there was only sand and sand and more hot and dry sand.

Serge had managed to rent a couple of apartments for us and the other members of our team. We lived on the first floor of one of those apartments on a very busy corner; the front road led to the old Crater center and the one on our other side led to the harbor. Lots of traffic. We had rented out our apartment in Amsterdam furnished, so for here we bought some furniture to tide us over. We soon settled in. I managed to find a nice houseboy to clean the house. He was even ready to do the cooking. His name was Abdul.

Abdul came highly recommended and turned out to be even better than I had hoped for. He always dressed in white, was about thirty years old and had a wife and two children back in the Yemen. Every once in a while, he would ask for one or two weeks leave and go visit them. He could earn much better money in Aden than he could at home.

I also hired a nanny for Mikey. She would have to do the laundry and look after the baby. Then came the trouble spot—who was going to clean the bathrooms and the toilets? Now we had to deal with the Indian caste system, which reigned supreme in these parts of the world. I finally found a young boy who was ready and willing to clean the toilets. When he didn't show up, guess who would be cleaning the toilets? Right, madame herself. Neither Abdul nor the nanny would touch the toilets. Well, I could live with that. In my young life I had had to deal with a lot worse than cleaning some toilets.

We soon started to meet some interesting people. One of those was a lady Serge had hired as his secretary. She was a British lady of around thirty-five, who was not only extremely efficient behind a desk and typewriter, but she was also a very enterprising lady. She loved riding CAMELS. One day we were invited to watch a camel race, and she was one of the contestants. Oh, how exciting it was to watch this. Those camels can run quite fast, but it was the viewing public that made it spectacular.

Each one had his or her own favorite rider and camel, and the cheering, the shouting, the guns that would go off in the air—it all made it somehow very special to be a part of. We tried to make as much noise as we could to encourage Patricia on her camel, but she did not win. She came in third. I should say, it was good that she did not win; I don't know how the

Arabs would have reacted if they had been beaten by a mere woman in a camel race! Now that she was simply an also-ran they were quite prepared to cheer her.

After the race, Patricia introduced us to a variety of people. Most of them were British military personnel. One of them was in charge of the training of cavalry horses. It seemed he also trained people who were interested in learning to ride. My ears perked up. Oh? That was interesting. I wanted very much to learn to ride a horse. My ambition did not go as far as camels; I left that to Patricia. Horses would do well enough for me.

CHAPTER SEVENTY-ONE

In which I am told to damn well mount my horse, with pants torn front to back.

As soon as I could, I arranged to get invited for a first lesson. I did not have riding breeches, so I used what I thought would be good enough for a first lesson. I did order some jodhpurs, though. The pants I was wearing were not stretchy by any means, but it was all I had. Women did not often wear pants in those days.

The first order of things was the introductions. Most of the others were wives of the British garrison personnel. The man in charge turned out to be very strict, loud, and bossy. That was fine by me; horses are very large animals and safety is a good precaution. Then he said, "Today, we are going to practice mounting and dismounting. *Oh, oh,* I thought. *That is going to be tough with these pants.* I was right. The first time I managed to get on the horse I heard a funny noise coming from my pants. I ignored it, glad I had reached the saddle of the horse.

"All right. Now we are going to dismount and then mount again."

Oh, no, that is not good, I thought. But it had to be done. I managed to get off the horse somehow without mishap, but when I tried to mount again, I heard a ripping sound and knew that my pants had just split down the middle. What to do? I just did not want to have to lift my leg and show everybody my pink undies! Then it came.

"Now, dismount, then mount up again."

I remained in the saddle.

He immediately pounced on me. "Why are you not getting off?"

"I have a good reason. Please, let me stay in the saddle this time." I said.

He at once roared, "No, when I say, dismount, then mount again, you do what I have instructed you to do!"

Now my back was up; I was not a member of the British troops. "Well, if you must know, I ripped my pants front to back!" I shouted right back.

For an instant, he was taken aback, but not for long. "Lady, I don't give a damn about your pants; when I say dismount, you dismount. Do you hear?"

"Yes, I hear. Everybody can hear because you are yelling at me!" Now I could see shocked faces all around me. I guess they were not used to anyone disobeying an order given by this lout.

I had a choice. I could get off my horse and leave, or swallow my pride and do what he said.

I did want to learn to ride a horse. I swallowed my pride, threw the lout a dirty look, and came off my horse. Then, with the rest of them, I mounted again, hoping that everybody had discreetly looked somewhere else but knowing they wouldn't; guess they were curious to know the color of my undies. Now we could finally start riding the darn horses.

Another time we were invited for dinner by the representative of the large BP oil company for whom we were building the three oil tanker bunker islands. (*Aden was actually the largest oil bunkering port in the whole world at the time.*) They lived in a palatial house, which was lovely to behold. I looked around with interest at all the things on display. Many Indian artifacts, ancient African ivory statues, vases from China, I loved it all. I guess they had done a lot of travelling.

There were about twenty guests. I knew she would have many servants to do the hard work, but still, the lady of the house is in charge and has to make sure everything is in order and done the way she wants it done. I expected her to be glad to be able to sit down and just converse with her guests. No, not her. She sat down and said, "This is the first day I have been able to really relax. It has been such a busy time for us."

She had twenty guests for dinner, yet she had been able to relax??? My goodness, I wondered what a busy day would be like for her. Maybe having a hundred guests, including maharajas and presidents, for a sit-down dinner? I felt quite humbled. I was twenty-seven years old and having twenty guests for dinner seemed like a huge undertaking to me, servants or not. I had a lot to learn.

CHAPTER SEVENTY-TWO

*In which I try to get pregnant again
but nearly choke to death.*

It stands to reason that I wanted to have another child, but I did not make a drama of it this time. I had discovered, during visits with the other ladies of our company, that there was a good method to get pregnant. It involved taking your temperature rectally every morning, then noting down the exact temperature. Usually towards the middle of the month the temperature would go up slightly. That would be a good time to try for a baby. So, as soon as I found the temperature had gone up, I would ask Serge to have sex with me, even if it was during siesta time when it was very hot. We did have air-conditioners in all the rooms, except the kitchen. (Yes, cooking was a very hot job. Abdul did not mind; he was used to it.)

The first month we had no success, but the next month I missed my period. Serge and I were pleased that it had gone so easily this time. We wanted a little girl. Serge had gotten his wish as Mikey had green eyes and very blond hair, whatever there was of it as yet. I wanted a girl with Serge's hair (his was very dark and curly) and dark eyes. We settled down to enjoy the experience; this time without all the anxiety we had with the first baby.

KISMET

Well, there are always times when anxiety can knock on your door, as was the case here. One day, Serge had gone to work early in the morning, and I had gone to the beach club with Mikey. While there, I had noticed some red spots appearing here and there, and I wondered why they were there. A while later, I noticed that there were many more red spots now. I decided it was time to go home and find out what was going on. I collected all our stuff, returned sunglasses and shoes that Mikey had 'stolen' from other tables, and alerted the driver to take us home.

Serge, Mikey, and I at the Beach club.
Check out the heavy metal fencing against the sharks.

I had suffered from bad throat aches during the last few months, and had received medication from the British doctor at the hospital. That morning I had taken two of those pills before I had anything to eat, but I did not think that could be the reason for the red spots. Then I started to swell up from the neck up; my eyes, my tongue, my lips, everywhere. I had trouble breathing properly and was now definitely scared. I dragged Mikey upstairs to my neighbor and asked her to take care of him. She backed off when she saw me. "What is wrong with you?"

"I don't know. I am going to phone Serge to bring the doctor here," I said, through my swollen lips.

I managed to get hold of Serge, and he came with the doctor within the shortest possible time. The doctor examined me and asked all kinds of questions. When I mentioned the pills and showed them to him, he said, "There is your answer. You are allergic to sulfa and should never take it without first eating a decent meal." I hadn't realized that; I now did remember always having my breakfast first, though, before taking the pills. By now, I could barely breathe; it was horrible. The doctor gave me a strong anti-histamine shot and the swelling slowly went down. It had been a really nasty experience. Serge went to our upstairs neighbor to explain what had been wrong, and to bring Mikey home.

She (our neighbor) had also gotten pregnant, using the same method we had used. She also had a little boy of Mikey's age and we often went to the beach club together. We could not go to the open beaches as the danger of sharks was very real. At the club they had put a strong metal fence around the beach area that went all the way down to the bottom. On the left side a kind of sea wall of big rocks had been created. If I took my eyes off Mikey even for a second, I would know where to find him: climbing those dangerous rocks! Well, boys will be boys.

CHAPTER SEVENTY-THREE

In which our local political situation gets worse, and Kennedy gets assassinated.

In October of 1963 we were all shocked to hear that Sir Kennedy Trevaskis, the high commissioner, had only just escaped with his life when a grenade had been thrown at him at the airport. One senior British official had not been so lucky; he was actually killed when the grenade exploded. Several civilians had also been killed, and over forty people were wounded in this event. This was the start of a terrorist campaign against British troops and civilians alike. It was a very unsettling time.

We were living on this very busy street with many apartment buildings. On the street level of the buildings there were shops, and people from all over the world and all walks of life could be seen walking along the sidewalks. In the building next to ours, there was a little restaurant on the street level. One evening there was a loud explosion; the next day we found out that some rebels had thrown a bomb into the restaurant. It damaged the building severely and the street was broken up, even as far as our building.

Mikey's first recognizable spoken word was "compressor"— he pronounced it as "compwessow," of course. He learned it because for days on end, compressors were breaking up the damaged pavement below our windows. Not a fun sound. After this event, we were more cautious about going outside in the streets. The rebels would not know that we were not British and were not members of the police force. But anyway, they just wanted to get rid of all outsiders and have independence for themselves. And look what independence brought them. I cringe every time I read about what else the inhabitants have to suffer and endure. So many people there have lost their lives, their jobs, their income, and have not much hope for a better future. And the fighting for independence continues.

And there was more bad news, but this time it was not local. It was November 22, 1963 that we heard the news over the radio that President John F. Kennedy had been assassinated. We were so shocked and sad and angry. Why would anyone want to kill that young president, who had so ingeniously and bravely solved the Cuban Missile Crisis not long before? It had only happened on October 14, just five weeks before Lee Harvey Oswald shot him. The Cuban Missile Crisis had been a dangerous confrontation between the U.S. and the Soviet Union during the Cold War. The whole world had held its breath, hoping that there would be no nuclear war. We had all been so relieved that it had been avoided. And now he was dead. It was a sad and difficult time, not only for us in Aden, but for people all over the world.

(*It made me think of Alexander II, Emperor of All Russia, who was assassinated by a bomb on March 13, 1881 in St.*

Petersburg, Russia. Twenty years earlier he had abolished the serfdom. The serfs were now free to leave the land they lived on. It had been something they had wanted for so many years, and this Tsar was able to give it to them. He too, was ready to do so much more for them. Now some rebels had killed him. I guess it was because Russia, too, was a troubled nation).

I suppose one should consider these first two events signs of difficult times. Everyone was still trying to adjust to a changing world after World War II. And we had to change with it. The work continued, here in Aden, but everywhere people were huddling together to talk about the dangerous local situation, as well as those in the rest of the world; no-one could be sure to be alive the next day. Everywhere there were fights for freedom from colonialism and heads fell. "Independence" was the slogan in those days.

CHAPTER SEVENTY-FOUR

In which we get caught in a very nasty sandstorm.

Life continued with its daily challenges, political or otherwise, but there were still very many happy moments. Mikey was, as always, "stealing" sunglasses and other interesting items from other people's tables at the Beach Club, which had to be returned (if I could figure out from where he had taken them). Serge joined us as often as he could. For a while it was very difficult for me to go to the bathroom there, as the cleaning fluids they used really made me want to throw up when I was in my first trimester of pregnancy. One day the three of us were there when Serge noticed a dark spot on the horizon. "I wonder what that is," he said thoughtfully. "I hope it isn't a sandstorm coming our way." With Ethiopia and Somalia right across from us, that was not unexpected.

We kept watching it, but then we got into a conversation with somebody who had dropped by our table. We chatted for a few minutes, and then suddenly, her eyes opened wide while she stared ahead. "What is that?" she said. We both turned to look too, and the little dot had become a huge black cloud that seemed to storm our way.

"Run for it!" shouted Serge. "That is a very bad sandstorm!" He grabbed our stuff, and sent me to the washroom with

Mikey where we would be safe while he got the car as close as he could get it.

I tried not to get sick from the smell, but it was so hot in the washroom that I was sweating buckets and almost didn't make it, just the few minutes we were in there. Then Serge came and called us. We ran to our car through the now-blazing storm, Serge holding little Mikey. I thought we were doomed; the storm was so strong that it was difficult to move forward in the direction of the car. Everyone else was in the same boat. Just trying to reach our cars was almost impossible.

We got in finally, but once in, we could not open the windows. It was stifling hot and it was difficult to breathe, but it was impossible to open the windows. Serge wanted to start the car but I was scared. "Serge, don't. We will be blown away when we start driving!"

He waited a moment but then he said, "We have to risk it; we are in even more danger here."

He drove slowly at first, then increased the speed. "Better this way, I think!" He had to shout because the storm was so loud all around us. The sand hit the car and the strength of the wind was such that the whole car wobbled back and forth. Little Mikey was very interested in the whole process. He squealed in delight when the whole car shook in all directions.

When we finally made it out of the storm, I was shaking; it had been very frightening. Nature certainly can throw it at you, and so unexpectedly. The next day we found out that fresh fish from the open seas had been found many miles inland. All the chairs and tables and umbrellas at the club had suffered a lot of damage and many of them were also found miles inland, but then in pieces. What an adventure that had been, but not one I wanted to repeat any time soon.

When I was around six months along, I found out during one of my regular visits to the doctor, that the baby had turned the wrong way around. She told me that if the baby did not turn back soon into the right position, I should have to have a caesarean section when the time came. She suggested it might be better for me to go back to Amsterdam (she knew we had an apartment there) and have the baby in the hospital there. "You could stay here, of course. We can do a caesarean for you, but I am sure the hospital in Amsterdam will be much better."

Oh, why did I listen to her! The baby did not turn around, and just before my seventh month Serge took Mikey and myself to the airport. He was not pleased to let us go away, but he agreed with the doctor that it would be better for me to have the baby in Amsterdam. I did not want to go but they insisted, so I went.

I was happy to see my parents again, and they were thrilled to see their little Mikey again. I had a photo of my parents, which I showed every night to Mikey. I would tell him about Opa and Oma and how much they wanted to see him. I even made him kiss the picture so that he would get the feeling that they were people that should be kissed. He did not remember them, of course; he had only been one year old when we went to Aden.

CHAPTER SEVENTY-FIVE

In which I have to have another Cesarean, but have a beautiful baby girl.

We had a long and arduous journey back to Holland. We had to land in Baghdad for an hour. I had Mikey on a leash, and was carrying a diaper bag in the other hand. I was exhausted from restraining the little rascal, and was huffing and puffing with my heavy belly. That little boy had so much energy, and wanted to touch and feel everything. Needless to say, I absolutely adored every inch of him. We finally landed in Schiphol airport. I soon spotted my parents and as quickly as we could we went to embrace them. Opa took Mikey in his arms and hugged him. Mikey had no objections; Opa was all right. But then came Oma's turn.

She tried to hug and kiss him while the tears ran down her cheeks; she was so happy to see him. But Mikey was not pleased. He said, "Oma no good!"

We were all stunned. I did not know how to excuse what he had said. Finally, I found the magic words; "Oma has a nice cookie for you. Would you like that?"

Mikey did not like milk but he certainly liked cookies. He looked at Oma a bit doubtfully, but then he nodded. Yes, he would not mind to have a cookie from Oma. She gave him a cookie and quickly grabbed him for a hug; he let her do her thing without complaining. Pfffft, that had been a very tough start to our stay. One reason Mikey might have been a bit repelled by Oma was probably because she had nervous tics in her face. Another souvenir of the years in the camps.

My parents were going to stay at my apartment (the renters had gone), so Mikey and I would not be alone. My dad also worked at the Main Office now, so it was quite handy for him. I went to see my doctor and told him the whole story. He was a very nice doctor; I liked him a lot. He examined me and said, "Yes, the baby is still in the wrong position, but it might still turn around. However, we will let you have it in the hospital because there you will be able to get all the help you will need.

(I will not go into great details about the baby's birth because it is too hard to even write about it, even after so many years).

On the 4th of May, 1964, in the evening, I started to have pains and the water soon broke while I was still at home. My dad drove me to the hospital and was told that they would let him know at home when the baby's birth was imminent. A friend of mine was going to stay with me as long as they would let her.

The same thing happened that had also happened with Mikey; the baby just would not go down into the birthing canal. Early in the morning came the call "Caesarean!" I was relieved because I already knew I could not have a normal birth. When I came to, my parents were there and a nurse brought in my baby. It was a beautiful girl with dark strands of hair. She also weighed well over eight lbs. I was so happy to see our little Tatiana. That was how we had decided to call a little girl. Cables were sent left and right, and Serge was delighted.

It was still the habit to keep women in the hospital for ten days after a caesarean. I had tried to feed the baby myself while she was in my room, but she did not respond well. I started to get very worried and told the nurse. She grumbled, "All these new moms just don't have any patience!" She was not very helpful; I did not know who to talk to.

When they came to collect the baby to take to the night room for babies, I hated to see her go. She was crying all the time and nobody seemed to be able to tell me what was wrong with her. My parents were visiting me on day-nine when the door was thrown open and a young nurse appeared. "If you want to see your baby alive you better come now; she is dying."

We ran to where they kept her. I saw her difficulty in breathing and knew that it was true; she was going to die. I kept my hand on her body, and stared at her for a long time, my parents by my side and tears running down my face. Then she sighed and breathed no more.

I kept saying "I will get over this. I will get over this" not knowing how I ever could. My dad had sent a telegram to Serge. "Tatiana seriously ill stop come." When he came, he was told that she had died. He was devastated. He embraced me for a long time, but there was nothing he could say. Tatiana had been nine days old.

CHAPTER SEVENTY-SIX

In which we are told to sue the hospital but we decline.

My doctor told us what had actually happened. After a caesarean the lungs of the baby have to be thoroughly cleaned. Her lungs had not been cleaned well enough, and she had developed pneumonia. Penicillin could not help her fragile body anymore; it had been too late when they discovered the cause. He said, "You know, you could sue the hospital. It was clearly their fault."

Both Serge and I shook our heads, "Suing them would not bring back our baby."

That was the tragic tale of our second baby. We had already loved her so much during my pregnancy; it was unbearably hard to lose her. My dad and Serge took her to her grave alone. They had decided that I was not strong enough to go with them, and my mother was looking after little Mikey. How does one get over such a loss? I was so grateful to have little Mikey. He kept coming to kiss me, because he must have felt that Mom was not herself.

A few days later, a couple from our Mersin days came over to visit us. They had big smiles on their faces and she carried flowers and a baby present. "We have come to see the new baby," they said.

I just stared at them, and could not get a word out. Then I burst into tears and said, "She died!"

They were so upset for me and for Serge; they knew how much we had wanted Michael and had been happy for us when they had heard about the new baby. And then they had to hear this sorry tale.

We had a good visit with them, in spite of the sad news we had to give them. We could tell them everything that had happened. They listened with so much sympathy that it made our hearts a little lighter. I still have all the letters and telegrams of sympathy that we received later. It really helped to know that we were not alone in our sorrow.

Serge returned a week later to Aden. Mikey and I followed two weeks later. I dreaded the reaction of the other women, and made up my mind to act as if nothing had happened. Wrong choice, of course. I heard later that they thought I had no heart because I was not crying all the time. My upstairs neighbor had had a healthy and beautiful baby girl that I had to admire, of course. Do knives cut? Not as much as this visit cut me. And all the later ones and every time she excused herself to "feed the baby."

At such times one is inclined to say "Why me? Why does this have to happen to me? I learned to say, "Why shouldn't it happen to me? What is so special about me that I should not have my share of great grief?"

CHAPTER SEVENTY-SEVEN

In which I become a pariah and even the pyramids don't look good. All because I want to pee.

December 1965. We were returning to our home in Amsterdam. We had been working very hard on the plans for our new property while in Aden, and we were very much looking forward to starting the construction of the house. But first we were taking the boat to Marseille, France, where we were going to pick up our new Mercedes. We had ordered it from Aden. It was a 220 model, and we loved it. We were meeting my parents in St. Moritz, a high resort town in the Swiss Alps. We were going to spend Christmas there together.

The ship we took from Aden came from Australia, and had many Italian returning immigrants on board, who were going to Italy on a vacation. Serge and I discussed how we would deal with the major stops. We did not want to leave our precious little Mikey in any one's else's hands, so we were going to divide the shore excursions. I wanted very much to see the pyramids, and Serge wanted to see the Acropolis in Athens.

After the ship went through the Red Sea—very warm, of course—we got to Suez. I got off the ship as per instructions. That meant that I had to be ready to go ashore at seven p.m. I had a quick breakfast, went to the bathroom for a quick pee, and was ready to go ashore. Once we were ashore, we just stood around on the dock, waiting for the bus that would bring us to Cairo. There was nowhere to sit, and we all began to grumble a little at the delay. A while later, I started to think that I should not have had that second cup of tea.

I looked around for anywhere where there could be a bathroom, but there was nothing. Just when I had decided to go up the gang plank to board the ship again to pee, we were all called to step into the bus which was just arriving. We all boarded the bus like little lambs. I was sitting next to a young Italian fellow who did not speak a whole lot of English. (How on earth did he manage to live in Australia and not learn to speak the language?)

I had no idea how long it would take to get to Cairo but I hoped it would not be too long; I really had to pee. I should have checked this before I left, because we were driving endlessly, it seemed, with the desert on both sides of the road. The bus was obviously not a new specimen because it creaked and groaned regularly. I was intrigued to see caravans of camels go by near to the road, but the urge to pee grew and grew.

Finally, I got up and went to speak to the driver. Above his head there was a sign that read: DO NOT SPEAK TO THE DRIVER. My need was too urgent; I saw no way out. I said, in my best high-brow English, "I would like to spend a penny." Every English person will know that this means that I need to go the bathroom. It was rather naïve of me to think that a simple Arab driver would understand me, but my need was so high I had to try.

He did understand the word penny, though. He said "Lady, you wait till Cairo. Then you spend lots of pennies!"

In desperation I finally blurted out my need. "I need to pee! Now!"

"No, no, lady. You wait till Cairo."

"No, no, no! You stop NOW!"

He was so taken aback by my shouting that he stopped the bus. I scrambled for the door with forty or more pairs of eyes upon me. I looked around. There wasn't a bush to be had, nothing, just flat, only slightly undulating desert land. Okay, this is it then. Fortunately, I was wearing a fairly wide skirt. I spread it around me, removed my undies discreetly, and peed. This must have been one of the most liberating and beautiful moments of my entire life! What a relief. Indescribable.

Did they turn their heads away to spare my blushes? Of course not! They hung out of the windows in order not to miss one moment of my shame. With a light heart and a happy smile, I stepped back into the bus. No smiles there, just accusing looks. Oh well, I deserved it, but it was well worth it. Little did I know what a catastrophe I had unleashed. Because the bus driver started the engine, but nothing happened; the engine would not start. No matter what he tried, he could not get that bus going again.

There they were—well over forty people sitting, standing, roaming round, stranded in the desert because of me, all throwing me dirty looks. Nothing to eat, not much to drink, I deserved all those nasty looks. I tried to make myself smaller and smaller, but what could I do? One thing did please me, though. Most of them now resorted to doing what I had done; they peed in the desert. In public. Another bus came by and promised to send another bus by as soon as possible. Some of the people were taken to Cairo by passing taxis, which had some room, and eventually we all arrived there. We were taken to the Cairo museum but it was hard for me to take anything in.

After that, we were taken to the Great Pyramid. We were offered camels and small horses and some donkeys to ride on, but by the time they came to me I had to be satisfied with a little old donkey; the others had all taken the best animals. I was the pariah, so a donkey was good enough for me. It was not exactly a highlight of my life, that trip. That pee of mine certainly did not do me any favors. But such is life. These things can happen. I decided to just take it as another adventure, albeit not a very successful one.

CHAPTER SEVENTY-EIGHT

In which Mikey disappears

When I told Serge the whole story, he laughed; that dirty so and so. He had no sympathy for me whatsoever. Yes, I guess it was sort of funny, but not funny ha, ha for me. Serge, however, had a great time visiting the Acropolis; he talked about it for days. I was glad he, at least, had had a good time. I was content to spend time with my beloved little boy.

Mikey did give us a scare, however. He would have his meal before we had ours and we would wait in the cabin until he was asleep, and then we would go and have our dinner. We had asked the stewardess to look in on him as often as she could. We could not lock the cabin door from the outside so it had to stay open, but we took turns to run down to check up on him.

It turns out he had not been completely asleep when we left. When we came down to check up on him, he was nowhere in sight. We panicked, of course. I ran upstairs because that was my worst fear; the railing, the ocean. Oh, my goodness, was I scared. You moms will feel my fear. No-one had seen anything, so I ran down again. They thought he might have gone down into the bowels of the ship. As we all came down, we were met by a sailor who carried Mikey in his arms. They had found him down near the engine room. He was crying, and had been asking for his "Mem-sahib." "I want my Mem-Sahib," he kept saying. Abdul always referred to me as his Mem-Sahib, so our little boy had probably reasoned that this was the best way to find me. I hauled him into my arms, hugging and kissing him, and thanked the sailor, tears of happiness and relief on my face. We found another way to have dinner, and never let Mikey out of our sight again.

Next stop was Marseille. We spent one night there, and walked around to admire all the lovely flowers and little parks in the area. The weather was perfect. Cool, but sunny. The Mediterranean was bluer than ever and sparkled in the sunlight. The next day we drove to the Mercedes dealership to pick up our new car. It was really beautiful. We had chosen a dark-red color and we loved it.

To drive to St. Moritz was almost 900 km so we stopped somewhere on the way for the night. *St. Moritz* is a high Alpine resort town in Switzerland, at an elevation of about 1,800 metres (5,910 ft) above sea level. We were really looking forward to showing Mikey the snow; he had not seen snow yet. At least, not while he was old enough to take it in and remember it.

As we approached St. Moritz, there was more and more snow beside the road. The closer we came, the higher the walls of snow got. Mikey wanted to get out, of course, to touch the snow. He was squealing with delight when he did, but soon said, "Mikey go in car; snow too cold." Serge and I laughed. So young, yet already so determined. Well, who could blame us for adoring him; we had waited for him long enough.

Seeing my parents again was a joyous occasion. Mikey had learned by now that Oma was his devoted slave, so he hugged her readily back. Opa had never been a problem; Mikey had liked him instantly. We had a great time there, dining together every night, and going out for all kinds of entertaining events, most of them for Mikey, of course, but Serge and I really looked forward to going back to Amsterdam. We had a house to build on our new property.

CHAPTER SEVENTY-NINE

In which a little Indian girl is tied to a tree and then forgotten by her captor and we find that the Al-Sabah family still rules Kuwait.

When we got home, Serge learned that he was going to be working on a project for Kuwait. Our company was designing a harbour for Kuwait. They also had to assist the Kuwaiti government to find another company, through adjudication, to build the harbour. Serge was first going to work on the design in Amsterdam, and then he would have to spend about eight or so months in Kuwait itself to finish the design. We were happy we could stay a while in Holland because we wanted to work on the design for our house. I was thrilled to go to Kuwait. I did enjoy this traveling around the world. It was exciting to see new places, and meet people with different habits and ideas, which really could only be done properly if one could stay in the country for a while.

I found a lady to clean my apartment once a week. I wanted to spend a lot of time visiting my parents and going to see our new property in Bosch en Duin *(Forest and Dune)* near Bilthoven and Zeist in the heart of Holland. I placed Mikey in a Montessori school for three-year-olds. He would go there three times a week for a few hours. I thought he needed to learn to be with other kids. At home he was quite spoiled, although we tried very hard not to spoil him too much. Meeting other children would teach him that the world did not really revolve around him alone. He actually liked going there, and for his fourth birthday party we invited six little friends to celebrate it with him.

Early January, we packed our bags, and said goodbye to Opa, Oma, and little Janine, who had become a very good friend of our Mikey. Remember, they had met when she was in her playpen at one year old and he was two. She cried buckets when he left and Mikey was not far off either. He loved having her follow him everywhere.

On one occasion, they had been playing cowboys and Indians. She had been the Indian that was tied to a tree and Mikey was the big cowboy who was going to save her. Then Mikey had to pee and therefore ran inside to do his business. On the way out, he got sidetracked by something that was playing on the television, and he settled down to watch it, forgetting all about the little Indian girl bound to the tree.

A little later it dawned on my mother that Janine was not with him. "Mikey, where is Janine?"

He looked up with shock on his face. His little hand flew to his mouth. "Outside, Oma."

She ran out and found a bitterly crying little Indian girl, still tied to the tree. Mikey followed my mom outside and hugged Janine. "I forgot, Janine," he said apologetically. She only cried harder, and Mikey had his hands full to get her in a better mood. Oma solved the problem by giving them both a bowl of chips; they happily nibbled away and peace was restored. But then the time came to leave Holland once again.

Kuwait actually only began its career early in the eighteenth century. A group of families of the Anizah tribe from the Arabian Peninsula migrated to the area that is now Kuwait. In 1756 they decided to appoint a sheikh from the Sabah family as their autonomous leader, thus creating an autonomous sheikhdom, which became Kuwait. Somewhere along the line, Sheikh Mubarak the Great, who had come into power by assassinating his brother, had been afraid of being annexed by the Ottoman Empire, which had been in power for a long time. He now sought a closer relationship with Britain. After the start of WWI, Kuwait became a British Protectorate.

In 1938 they found OIL! This was great for Kuwait, but now Iraq put in a claim that Kuwait was actually part of its lands, citing an old rule. In June 1961, Britain finally decided to recognize Kuwait's independence while Iraq kept pushing to annex Kuwait. In the end, Iraq had to admit defeat; they recognized Kuwait's independence and its borders. The Al-Sabah family was still in power at the time when we came to Kuwait.

CHAPTER EIGHTY

"In which you get a history lesson, Mikey watches Hercules in Arabic, and Naim kisses my feet.

What was much more exciting to me was the fact that Kuwait, situated at the tip of the Persian Gulf, had been the site where our earliest known civilization suddenly blossomed around seven to eight thousand years ago. The biblical Abraham was born in Ur, a city close to the river Euphrates. Just imagine, in the year 2033 BCE, Abraham was born in the very same place where we were going to be living for the next eight months. And desert views do not change, not even over thousands of years. We would see what Abraham saw four thousand years ago!

What is the country of Iraq today, used to be the land called Mesopotamia, which means "Land between Two Rivers." The two rivers were the Euphrates and the Tigris. And, as is evident, the city of Ur is located in or near the place where Kuwait is today. Nearby Eridu was the oldest city of the entire area. Its so-called god was Enki; he had started to build the city of Eridu about six or seven-thousand years ago, if not earlier. The entire area of Mesopotamia is telling us a fascinating story about our civilization and what happened during the last 8000 years or so.

The land of Sumeria was the place where the first cities were built, where the wheel was invented, where writing was developed, where mathematics were created, and where they first developed the sexagesimal counting system, which is still used for many things today. They gave the circle its 360 degrees, divided the year into twelve lunar months, and they knew a great deal about astronomy. They even gave our planets their own names, which we never knew about until about one hundred years ago when the famous archaeologist Leonard Woolley started to take a closer look at all things Sumerian.

My question has always been **"WHO TAUGHT THEM THESE THINGS?"**

If we assume that there really was a Great Flood, caused by a devastating comet that struck our planet nearly 13,000 years ago, we must assume that most people living on earth at the time, were also destroyed. Remember Atlantis? Could a remnant of these people, as a new theory states, have been the ones that helped to create our present civilization? This theory has not yet been accepted by mainstream scientists, but it does make sense. If you have a better idea please let me know; I am very interested to find out the truth.

In the meantime, this area was really interesting to live in. Several of our people went to visit cities like Baghdad with its museum of antiquities. I would have loved to go, but Serge was just too busy and could not get away. Babylon is the most famous city from ancient Mesopotamia and lies only fifty-nine miles southwest of Baghdad. It was easy to visit the ruins for those lucky folks who did go. I wish I could do those years again. I am certainly not complaining, but I did so enjoy living in all those exotic places.

I spent my days going to the beach with Mikey, shopping for groceries, reading, and having visits with the other ladies and their children. Some of those couples who went with us to Kuwait are still my very great friends. We often were invited for dinner parties, or just cocktail parties with other foreigners like us. We never did get to know any real Kuwaitis; they had very strict rules about their wives. Serge met many Kuwaiti men, but they kept their women at home.

Serge had found us a house in the outskirts of Kuwait. There was a row of these houses, but there was no real street, as I remember it. Just desert sand, by now hard-packed. Several English couples lived in the same area, and Mikey went to a pre-school one of those ladies had started. Mikey was allowed to play outside with other children, some of them Arabic. He loved visiting them because they had television. The children often watched cartoons and Mikey loved that. He saw *Hercules* in Arabic! Now I think, *How could I let him go outside and visit homes I did not know the people of?* But everybody did the same with their children; I guess it just was the norm at the time.

We had a little one-room building attached to the right of our house, to be used by a cook or houseboy. We hired a young Palestinian man, who spoke some very limited English. He would cook and clean the house. His name was Naim (na-eem).

He was very proud, as most Arabs are. He and I often clashed, but we usually resolved the problem. One time we didn't. He shouted, "I shall leave this house and I shall never come back!"

I was very happy to hear that, actually. I had been trying to find a way to get rid of him, because he really was a rather difficult man to deal with. I said, "Go, Naim, go! There is the door. Now give me back my key."

He slammed the key on the table, turned, and stalked out. His face was red with fury. I locked the door behind him and sighed with relief. Finally, I'd gotten rid of him.

He was a Palestinian and very involved with the Palestinians living in Kuwait. He was always talking about the day when the Jews would be kicked out of their land, which would then again become his homeland, Palestine. It made us really uneasy to have him in the house with us.

Two hours later there was a knock on the door. I said, "Who is there?"

"It is Naim, Madame."

"Why are you here?"

"Please, Madame, I want to come back and work for you again."

"No, Naim. You left because you could not work for me anymore!"

"I am sorry, Madame. I do want to work for you again. Please, Madame, let me in." He was speaking so loudly that I was afraid the whole neighborhood could follow the conversation. He started banging on the door.

I did not know what to do, so I let him in again. I opened the door, walked into the living room, and sat down. He followed me, kneeled in front of me, and started kissing my feet, while begging over and over again to let him work for me again. I kept shaking my legs free from his kisses, and finally said in desperation, "All right, all right! You can come back again."

Now he was happy. He swore I would not regret this decision and that he would be the best houseboy I had ever had.

CHAPTER EIGHTY-ONE

In which Naim finds a scorpion on his naked shoulder and my attempts at making alcohol work much better than they should.

We had more adventures with Naim. One day he came in with a white face and shaking all over. "What happened, Naim? Sit down, sit down." I thought he would fall over from shock, or whatever the reason was for his condition.

He said, "Madame, I woke up, opened my eyes, and saw this big scorpion sitting on my naked shoulder. I know these scorpions; they are deadly."

"Oh, how awful! What did you do?"

"I flicked it off my shoulder, hoping it would not get me first. Then I found it and killed it good and dead. Then I ran here. I am sorry, Madame. I got really scared." He was close to crying. Of course, he was scared, poor man. That was a terrible thing to have happened to him.

I made him a cup of coffee with lots of sugar and something to eat and told him to just sit and relax. He had had a terrible shock and his body had to get back to normal first. I was rather touched that he had run to me to tell his scary tale. I guess he did not really hate me, after all. On the other hand, where else could he have run? He had no real home in Kuwait. His family lived in the Gaza strip, one of the very few areas left to Palestinians.

Then one day, I had another weird thing happen. This one did not have anything to do with Naim, but with our desire to have alcoholic drinks. In Kuwait we could not buy liquor, of course, it being a Moslem country. But we did want to have parties with a little bit of alcohol, so we made it ourselves. I did too. I filled a special tub in the bathroom with fifteen liters of water, then added five kg of white sugar. This I was I supposed to leave sitting for a couple of days, after which the distillation process would be started. Someone had lent me all the right equipment.

We were going to have a party at our place, and that is why we needed the alcohol. We got the different tastes from Holland in tiny little bottles; rum, vodka, gin, etc. I would end up with one bottle of ninety-percent alcohol. This I would divide into three bottles. One would be used to make the alcohol taste like rum. We would just fill the rest of the bottle with purified water. The next one would get the gin taste, etc. We would end up with three bottles of booze, which could be used in mixers. I would usually end up doing two sessions to end up with six bottles. It was hard work in that heat! I did not want Naim to touch it, as he was a Moslem and did not approve of me making alcohol.

The first time I made it, I made a big mistake. The sugar was fermenting in the bathroom, in its tub with fifteen liters of water, and Serge and I went out to visit somewhere. Naim was going to sleep in Mikey's room. The bathroom was at the top of the stairs that led to the bedrooms. We came home around eleven p.m. and smelled something funny coming from the house. We looked at each other—what on earth could that funny smell be? It almost smelled like a distillery. Serge opened the door and started to laugh.

I did not laugh, I was horrified!

I had not checked the temperature of the water, which came from our roof. It would be brought in and pumped up onto the roof. Where it got nice and warm in the hot sun... My fermentation had been accelerated many times, by putting the sugar into fifteen liters of warm water. There was a stream of the stuff coming all the way down the stairs. Not nice, not nice at all, but I learned something again. Serge helped me clean up the mess, and we finally got to bed. Fortunately, Mikey slept through everything, and Naim would not know what had happened.

The party was a great success, and we danced happily for hours with our friends and others we had invited for this occasion. We had to create our own entertainment, as there were few things to do for us foreigners outside of our homes. And it created a lot of goodwill all around.

CHAPTER EIGHTY-TWO

This is all about the six-day Arab-Israeli War.

The Six-Day War was fought between 5 and 10 June 1967 by Israel and the neighboring states of Egypt, Jordan, and Syria. For months there had been talk about the possibility of war erupting between Israel and Egypt. Kuwait was a Moslem country, so foreigners had to be very careful in their statements. Most of us felt for Israel, as it was surrounded by Arab countries. It became known that Egypt, Jordan, and Syria had formed a coalition. Ever since the Israeli victories in the wars of 1948 and 1956, everyone knew that a third clash could be expected. Serge and I just hoped it would not happen while we were there.

We had arrived in Kuwait in early January and were expected to stay until October or so, in order to finalize the details of the plans for the new harbour that our company was designing for the Kuwaiti government. We had felt the explosive mood in the city all along, and that is why we were not happy to have Naim as our houseboy. He was actually one of the leaders in Kuwait of the large Palestinian club. And he was very vocal in his opinions.

(Israel had been Palestine, until the United Nations voted in 1947 to split the British-controlled area of Palestine into two sections. One for the Palestinians and the other for the Jews, so they would not fight each other anymore. Hundreds of thousands of Jews had been resettled in British Palestine after WWII and the Palestinians had fought the influx tooth and nail. The British had been unable to stop the violence. The area left to the Palestinians had been roughly twice the size of the area given to the Jews. Today, the Jews have taken over most of Palestine, so it is not surprising that the Palestinians feel very strongly that they have been given a very rough deal).

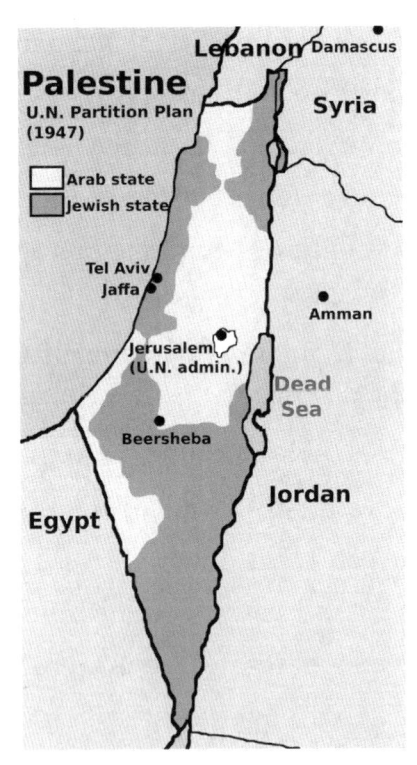

**Original plan of division of Palestine:
Yellow for Palestinians and blue for Israel.**

Later, we found out that Russia had falsely informed Egypt that eleven to thirteen Israeli brigades intended to attack Syria.[6]

In response, Egypt started concentrating forces along the border with Israel and on May 16 demanded that the UN peace-keeping forces leave the peninsula. Israel also refused the presence of UN peace-keeping forces on their side of the border. Then Egypt, Jordan, and Syria started mobilizing their forces along Israeli borders. Iraq sent forces, and Saudi-Arabia promised its support as well to Egypt, Jordan, and Syria.

Then, on the 5th of June we were warned that foreigners better stay indoors, because Israel had attacked Egypt and completely destroyed its air force. Naim came in, beside himself, and was so angry that Serge signaled me to stay clear of him as much as possible. Naim had hoped, of course, that Israel would be destroyed and that Palestine would be reinstated in that whole area.

On the one hand I felt for him. He wanted his old country back. On the other hand, he was so angry that I thought he would murder us in our beds, because the Arabs immediately said that the U.S. had helped Israel. Now all lighter-skinned people were suspect, and were in danger. I kept Mikey at home during the next week while the war lasted. I said to Naim that I was very sorry that he did not get his own country back yet, but I thought to myself that I could not blame Israel for wanting to defend itself by attacking first, being surrounded

---

6   Why would Russia do that? In The Spymaster, the Communist, and Foxbats over Demona, the authors thought that the Russians were intent on destroying Israel before it could obtain atomic weapons.

by so many hostile neighbors. We all had been so certain that Israel had no chance to win this war—that they would have been completely destroyed if they had waited for Egypt to start the war. This attack by Israel was a preventative attack.

After the war was officially over, the general feelings in the city were very divided. Some of us started to act as if nothing had happened, because here in Kuwait nothing had happened. Others were very sad, in the face of Egypt's loss of its air force and the loss of so many lives. After all, most of the people that lived in Kuwait were Moslems. Egypt had lost 15,000 people, Jordan had lost 700, Syria had lost 2,500, and Israel had lost 983. It was very sad to think of all those people losing their precious lives.

The Palestinians were still very, very angry and I must confess I never felt very safe anymore. Naim did not seem to take out his anger on us, and that was quite a relief. We were happy that he had assumed his normal attitude. Slowly, slowly, things started to get back to 'normal'. At least, back to the normal we had before the war exploded. Serge and his team got all the work done, and by the end of October the three of us could go back to our beautiful apartment in Amsterdam.

CHAPTER EIGHTY-THREE

This is all about horses, new friends, and neighbors.

It was nice to see my parents again and they soon went back to spoiling Mikey. Little Janine was happy to have her playmate back. And Serge went to work again at the Main Office. Before our Kuwait venture, Serge had been promoted to general-manager of the Associated Marine Consultants. The Royal Netherlands Harbour Works Company had been sold, and some of the directors had decided to just keep an engineering design company. That was the reason why our present company was only designing the harbour of Kuwait. A company from Yugoslavia actually built it.

Serge and I now actively started to work on our new house. We had hired an architect to make the official plans and oversee the construction of the house, but we went there as often as we could. We were going to call the house "Polanka," which meant "open place in the woods," or glade. Serge was a great admirer of Leo Tolstoy, who had a property called Yasnaya Polyana, south of Moscow. Polanka is sort of a diminutive of that name. Even today, people still flock to Tolstoy's property to admire it and the house where he wrote so many of his novels.

One day, when I came on my own to check up on the construction, I noticed that the kitchen window was not over the sink area. This was not in the plan; it was supposed to be over the kitchen sink. I asked the man who was working on it why it was not. He said, "Well, it just did not come out that way."

I was stunned. Even here checking up on the works was necessary? I high-tailed it over to the architect to tell him about this. He was horrified. "That imbecile! Of course, it has to go over the window sink! He was probably too lazy to cut the bricks." The problem was rectified, but our inspection trips became even more frequent!

In August of 1968 we finally moved into our new home; Polanka was beautiful. We had hired a gardener to put in the lawn and lots of plants and bushes and everything was really nice. Mikey was now almost seven years old and we put him in a Montessori school. He stayed there until it was time to go to high school. I did not really like the Montessori system. There was no competition at all. No need to make extra efforts, as they don't want any child to develop a complex if they can't keep up. It is a really good system, but I am afraid I am quite competitive, and I did not like the idea of just getting through the classes without having to make any extra effort to reach a higher level of learning. After some family discussions we all agreed that Mikey (Michael by now) would go to a regular high school in Zeist. He wanted to become a veterinarian and that meant six years of high school instead of the usual five.

We discovered a riding club nearby, and Michael wanted very much to learn to ride a horse. It was hard to see that little boy at seven years old climb on top of a 16.3-hand horse; they did not have ponies. I sat through every lesson he had and I trembled every time again when the horse would act up. Mike got thrown several times and oh, what went through my heart then.

I had also started riding again, and I soon met a nice woman with whom I often rode through the woods. We actually lived close to where Princess Beatrix (who later became the queen) had her residence in an area called The Laage Vuursche. She rode in the same woods and we would meet her sometimes with her entourage.

Michael and I started to think that we would like to have a horse of our own. I thought this was a marvelous idea, but we had to do some convincing before Serge decided to let us go for it. In fact, I told him that I would stop smoking (by now I smoked two packages of Pall Mall non-filter cigarettes a day) if he would let us buy a horse. Mike had been writing essays in school about how much his mother smoked; he so wanted me to stop smoking. I had felt more and more guilty about not being able to stop—I did try many ways—but it just didn't work.

Serge accepted my 'deal', and Mike and I started to look for a nice horse. We found one. She was a Budyonny. The Budyonny is a breed of horse from Russia. They were developed for use as a military horse following the Russian Revolution and are used as an all-purpose competition horse and for driving. She had been imported and used by someone who had put a wrong saddle on her back, resulting in her behaving badly when anyone tried to ride her. She was put out to pasture for six months and then she was put up for sale. She was a golden chestnut and we absolutely doted on her. Serge named her Dushka (darling). She quickly adjusted to Mike riding her, although she often bucked in the beginning. We soon got used to it and fell more and more in love with her. I, too, managed to ride her and felt very comfortable on her back.

Mike and Dushka learning cross-country jumping.

The lady I rode with—her name was Ruth—lived not far from us and we became good friends. She was actually Canadian by birth, married to a Dutchman who had come to British Columbia to buy wood. She told us a lot about B.C. and Vancouver and how there were many cattle ranches in B.C. Mike and I listened with rapt attention. Serge and I had talked so often about how wonderful it would be to live on a really large property. He was always talking about how great Raduzhnaya had been. How large the property had been; it made me almost jealous. All these stories Ruth told us made me think.

Our Canadian friend Ruth Bakker.

Serge decided that he would only work four days a week. This meant that he stayed home on Wednesdays. This was really nice; we enjoyed the extra day. We met some of our neighbors and visited back and forth. But there was one neighbor with whom things did not go very smoothly. She lived behind us. A lane next to our property led to her house.

We had bought an English Pointer; we called her Diana, and when she was a year old, we let her have puppies.

Our Diana on the best seat of the house.

One day, I was behind the garage, feeding Diana's ten puppies, when I saw the neighbour near her fence. I said, trying to be friendly, "Good morning; isn't it a lovely day?" We had not met yet.

Then she said in a very unpleasant tone, "Why have you never come to introduce yourself to me?"

"Why should I do that? I was expecting you to come to me to welcome me."

"I? I should come to you?! Why, don't you know that my family used to own all this land here?"

"No, I did not know that. That must have been wonderful for you. But where I come from people visit newcomers and bid them welcome."

"Well, I was waiting for you to show up and you never did. I was very insulted." I apologized for having unknowingly insulted her. Then I went over to the fence, stuck out my hand, and introduced myself, telling her how much I liked our property. I hoped this would mellow the lady a little. I did not want to have a feud with a neighbour.

Unfortunately, things did not work out so well after all, because the very next day Serge went to feed the ten little pointer puppies. He was standing next to a large plate with dog food and was surrounded by the puppies. He was enjoying their antics, but he was wearing just his pajama pants (and nothing much else) when some of the puppies pulled his pants all the way down. He laughed and pulled his pants up again, but then he noticed our neighbour. She was standing by the fence with an open mouth, outrage written on her face. Serge, never daunted, smiled graciously and said, "Good morning, Madam." Her mouth snapped shut, she turned around and walked away. Needless to say, we never became close friends!

CHAPTER EIGHTY-FOUR

In which I become involved with a tennis club, and someone falls out of a tree.

I looked around for a tennis club because Serge and I really enjoyed the game. He had been a great player when he was young, but everyone knew he hated to be beaten. Well, Serge was as passionate about tennis as he was about bridge, so who could blame him? Right! I became one of the founders of a wonderful tennis club close by and it kept me very busy organizing events and playing, of course.

We met a couple, Bill and Joyce, who had a boy Mike's age. They lived down the road from us. They were quite well-to-do (he also bought wood in Canada, like Ruth's husband did), and he liked to "live it up." After work he often would drop in on one of the many bars, and usually found some females to spend the time with. If Joyce voiced her objections to this behavior, he would say, "If you don't like it, there is the door!" They would somehow make up again, but it was, to say the least, a very volatile relationship.

They had recently had another baby, a girl, who was about six months old at the time. One day, Bill had not come home again and Joyce got her revenge. When he did not come home when he had said he would, she went to his favorite bar and

KISMET

found him. Next to him was a pretty young woman who looked up at him with adoring eyes. Joyce asked him, no doubt aggressively, when he intended to come home. He said, "You will see me when you see me." Joyce threw him a very nasty look, which should have warned him, turned around, and went back home.

Edie playing tennis at the club.

Around two a.m. she heard his car going into the garage. He tried getting in the front door with his key, but it was locked. He tried to get into the house through the garage, but it was also locked. He finally went around the house and tried the door to the kitchen. He was very pleased to find that it was open. He tried to step into the house, but Joyce came towards him with a pail full of diaper poop and threw it right in his face. Then she locked the door on him.

He yelled, shouted, screamed in anger but she would not budge. He finally managed somehow to scrub the poop off his face and everywhere else, then, wet as he was, he climbed back into his car and slept there. Joyce was very pleased with herself, but he was not very happy with her. It took a few days, but they stayed together. Unbelievable, but true.

They actually stayed together until he died. I don't know how they managed their lives, but they did. It sure does take all kinds to make this world go around, doesn't it? They were a good neighbors, though. Serge was in Kuwait, one time, when I discovered our Spotty under the dining table. She was dead. She had been almost fifteen years old. It was late at night. I did not know what to do about Spotty; I felt I had to do something for the poor little thing. I finally phoned Bill and Joyce. They both came immediately. Bill took Spotty away with him and said he'd look after everything. Joyce held my hand and consoled me. Such things one does not forget.

Michael and I liked to walk in the woods, while waiting for Serge to come home. Once there was a series on television about the origin of the River Nile. I told Michael that we should pretend to be in Egypt, looking for the origin of the Nile River. We took the dogs (we had sold eight of the puppies, but kept two males; Charley and Bamse (bear in Danish) and proceeded into the woods across from our house.

Mike kept running ahead to see if he could see the origin yet. Then I thought, *Why not make it even more exciting by letting him come back and not find me?* I found a nice tree and climbed up, thinking to really surprise him. Well, I really surprised him all right, but not in the way I had intended, for when I reached for a branch to climb higher, I felt the branch crumble in my hand. I fell. I managed to slightly turn my body but I landed hard and consequently screamed in pain.

Mike heard me and came running. "Mom, what happened? What happened?"

I had to admit that I had climbed the tree and had fallen down. "But I am getting up now, and then we can go home." The problem was, I could not get up. Mike tried to help me get up and I even managed a couple of steps but then I fell down again from the pain in my back.

Michael started to panic. "Mom, what shall I do now?" He was only ten years old and had never dealt with a real emergency, of course.

"I am afraid you will have to go get Daddy; he must be home by now."

He left, running.

CHAPTER EIGHTY-FIVE

In which I manage to get to the hospital and get a lesson in how to accept the modern world.

There I lay. The dogs thought it was a new game and kept jumping over me. It had begun to drizzle a little. I felt very annoyed with myself, but also a little sorry for myself, because it hurt so much. I did not dare to move even. There did not seem to be anybody else in the woods. I did not know how Serge could get me out of there. Finally, I heard the screech of an engine and our Mercedes came crashing through the bushes. Serge came rushing out of the car and asked, "Are you hurt? Are you in pain? What happened?" I told him. He said, "You climbed a tree?"

Yes, I had climbed a tree! And I was being punished for it, wasn't I?

When Serge had calmed down a bit, he tried to help me into the car. There was no way I could get up. Mike tried to help but he was only ten years old and that did not work either. Then we saw a gentleman coming, who was walking his dog. Serge asked him to help me into the car. They lifted me into the front seat and I hung there, tears in my eyes because it was so terribly painful. Serge loaded the dogs and Mike into the car, and we left to go to the hospital. I was biting my lips not to cry out at every move the car made, and hoped we would reach the hospital very, very soon.

Unfortunately, Serge had intended to get gas on the way back to town; he had had just enough to reach the house and get to the gas station. In all the worry and anxiety, he had forgotten that fact, but now he remembered. We had first to stop for gas, because he would not have enough to get to the hospital. I cried out in agony, but it had to be done. At long last we came to the hospital, and soon I was lying on a gurney and being wheeled inside.

A doctor bent over me and asked the fateful question, "So, what happened? Tell me all about it."

"Well, I fell out of a tree."

"You did what?!"

"I fell out of a tree. My son and I were playing a game, I climbed a tree, and fell out."

He smiled. "Oh, that explains it. We'll take some x-rays and then we can see what damage you did to yourself."

Serge and Mike stayed with me while we waited. Serge was very worried. I explained in more detail what Mike and I had been doing, and he laughed. "It certainly was a very educative way to entertain our son. But next time, leave the tree-climbing to your son, okay?"

"How could I know that that darn tree branch was dead? I was in such a hurry to hide from Mikey that I did not take the time to check."

The doctor came back with a nurse. "Well, you have broken several bones of your spinal column. Fortunately, nothing happened to the spinal cord itself; you got lucky, young lady!"

We were happy to hear that, but what would happen now?

"It means that you will have to lie flat on your back for six weeks. After that, you will have to learn to walk again, very slowly. It will be a long process. If you have help at home you can stay at home, but if not, we will have to keep you here in the hospital.

We considered it. Serge was working, Mikey had to go to school, and we had three dogs; our beloved English pointer Diana and her two sons, Bamse and Charley. No way could I stay at home, so the hospital it had to be.

Serge was going to make arrangements with Joyce to keep Mikey after school four days a week, and we had to think of what to do with the dogs. We were not going to part with Diana; she could stay with my parents, but we would have to sell Charley and Bamse. It was hard, but it had to be done. Trying to smile cheerfully, Serge and Mikey left, Serge promising to bring some of the stuff I would need, like books, clothes, etc. later that day.

After a while, I was wheeled into my room. The other bed was empty for now. I started think how nice it would be if someone would come and wash my face and my hands, which had become filthy with climbing the tree and falling out of it. My clothes were dusty too; in fact, I really needed to be tended to. But there was a worse dilemma; I needed to pee by now. A long time had passed since my last pee.

I looked around and found the bell. I tentatively pressed it, and soon after, a young man entered the room. He wore some kind of apron that looked almost like the ones the nurses wore. "Yes, what can I do for you?"

I was not pleased to see a man instead of a nurse, but I said, "Could you help me clean my face and hands, please? I feel so dirty."

He nodded, turned around, and came back with a wash cloth and a towel. He handed them to me. "There you are. Help yourself, dear." He looked at me with a smile and said, "Is there anything else I can do for you?"

I hesitated, then said, "Eh, no, no, thank you." I was too embarrassed to ask him to give me a bedpan. He left.

It was one thing to be too proud, or too embarrassed to ask for the bed- pan, but I did have to pee. And, I thought, there must be nurses in this hospital. I'd wait awhile, then ring the bell again. I was sure this time a nurse would show up. *What was that fellow doing here, anyway?* I asked myself irritably. I thought there were only female nurses.

I tried to think of other things, but it was no good. I had to pee, urgently. I pressed my bell again. The door opened and the same young fellow came into the room. He smiled broadly and asked, "Yes, what is it this time?"

I was not pleased. "Eh...eh, could I have a glass of water?"

He nodded, disappeared, and came back with a big glass full of water. "Here you are. That should help, don't you think?"

I thanked him politely, and he left the room again.

I cursed myself. Why was I so bashful? I obviously would never get a nurse here. I had to ask him for a bed pan, but everything in me screamed, no...no... no, not of him. I wanted a nice, kind, smiling woman to come to my rescue.

I heard some giggling in the corridor outside my room. Someone asked, "And, did she ask for the bed pan yet??"

More giggling followed, "No, she is still too abashed to do it, but she will have to learn that now there are male nurses too." I cringed. What had I done? Why had nobody told me that there would be male nurses? They should have warned me about this. I was getting more and more upset, with myself, with those in charge, and with the two giggling men nurses out there. One fact remained, though, I had to pee. I pressed the bell.

The door opened, but before he could say a word, I said, "Please bring me a bedpan."

He smirked, shoved the bedpan under me and said, "Anytime, my lady! Call me when you are done." Outside my door I heard him say, "She is learning...!" Yes, I had to accept another new way of the world. It should not be too hard; there had been so many already, hadn't there? But this one was really, really annoying.

CHAPTER EIGHTY-SIX

This is all about politics and the choosing of a country.

The political atmosphere in Holland had shifted towards the left, while we had been abroad. It got actually quite bad with people throwing rotten tomatoes at large cars, and more of such indignities. It was very unpleasant. We were certainly not rich, but we did have a nice car and a beautiful property, which we loved very much. It was hateful to feel the envy of the people everywhere. Serge had worked very hard for what we had; it had not come to him easily. Every day the news had new stories, and it got so bad that one day I said, "Why do we stay in Holland? Let's move to another country."

Serge and Mike looked at me questioningly. "Move where? This is your country." No, it is my father's country. Indonesia is my country, but there is no future for you there."

Mikey jumped up and said, "Let's go to Canada. They have lots of cowboys and Indians there, as Aunt Ruth was telling us."

Serge said, "If we have to go anywhere else, we should go to South-Africa; it is a beautiful country." He had been there on that good-will business trip and had loved every inch of the country."

"Oh no," I piped up. "If we have to go that far away then let's go to Australia. Talk about space; there is so much space on that continent that you sometimes have to travel for days without meeting another soul."

Well, which one would it be?

Serge and I had another drink. Now we really got into the spirit of things. Australia was really far away from everywhere; maybe that wasn't such a good idea. Then what about South-Africa? Serge proceeded to tell us how wonderful it was there—great climate, beautiful scenery all around, reasonable cost of household goods; he couldn't say enough good things about it.

"But," I said, "what about their apartheid system; that is not so nice, is it?"

South Africa's apartheid is a familiar concept the world over. But what did it actually look like? As Mark Byrnes asked in his article on "Life in Apartheid-Era South Africa," dated December 10, 2013. He writes:

> *"Established in 1948 under the racialist National Party, apartheid not only meant separate and inferior public services, benches and building entrances for non-whites. It also stripped South African blacks of their citizenship (placing them into tribally-based bantustans instead) and abolished all non-white political representation. A* **Bantustan** *(also known as Bantu homeland, black homeland, black state or simply homeland) was a territory set aside for black inhabitants of South Africa and*

South West Africa (now Namibia), as part of the policy of apartheid.

"Nelson Mandela was a key anti-apartheid activist, leading defiance campaigns and working as a lawyer. He was arrested in 1962, and given a life sentence for conspiracy to overthrow the government. His imprisonment did little to quell resistance. After years of violent unrest at home and sanctions abroad, the National Party began apartheid reform in the 1980s. In 1990 Mandela was finally released from prison and even had one turn as president in 1994."

When we discussed all these facts, it soon became clear that South-Africa was not the best of choices either, nice climate or not. We were only living in 1975 at the time, and Apartheid was still a nasty fact of life. Mike was jubilant. "Now there is only Canada left, so that is where we will go!"

Serge laughed and said, "Why not?"

I said, "I will phone the Canadian Embassy tomorrow."

And that is how the Canadian part of our lives was decided. When I came back with lots of information from the Canadian embassy and showed it to Serge, he was a little hesitant. "Wait a minute, aren't you going a little too fast here?" he said. "We have a beautiful house, we love living here, Mikey likes it, you have the tennis club, in which you are so involved, and Dushka.

I can play a lot of golf; why should we move? Just because the political atmosphere is not to our liking?"

We toyed with the idea over and over again, discarding it one moment, reviving it the next. Then we decided we would go to British Columbia and do a tour of the province to see whether we could see ourselves living there. We went there in August 1975. Michael was ecstatic!

CHAPTER EIGHTY-SEVEN

In which we travel through B.C., meet a drunken neighbor as well as two donkeys, and have a lovely campfire.

I had managed to get a copy of the British Columbia Real Estate book of the Block Brothers company. I had checked almost every listing in the book, and had been very surprised to find that all houses seemed to have been built of wood. In Holland, all houses were built of bricks. I kept looking for houses built of brick in the catalogue but could not find any. I asked Ruth Bakker about this, and she laughed. Of course, they are all built of wood; we have the most beautiful woods of Canada in British Columbia. We don't build with bricks, and even if we use bricks it is usually only to enhance one particular wall in a house. We don't make enough bricks to build the whole house.

In Holland there is a whole lot of good clay to be found along the rivers, so brick-making is indicated. In B.C. there is a lot of wood. Ergo, everything is built of wood. It took me a while to get used to this idea. We were going to take a month to travel through B.C., starting in Vancouver. We stayed in Vancouver for a few days, doing the sight-seeing tour of all things Indian for Mikey's sake. Well, by now we called him Mike, but to me he would always be Mikey.

We were so surprised to see how the houses were situated in Vancouver. Lovely tree-lined lanes had nice houses on either side of the road, which were maybe only six feet away from the next house. In Holland, those houses would be attached to save room for the next house. Here, that wasn't the case. Each house had to be individually built on its own little lot. I suppose they had a lot more space here in B.C. then we did in Holland.

Next goal was the town of William's Lake where the Stampede would have been held on the July 1 long weekend. We had booked a cabin at a so-called Dude-Ranch near to the town, and we really looked forward to going there. Michael was excited to see his first Indian. We had all the books by Karl May about Winnetou and Old Shatterhand. They both looked really good in the pictures.

On the way from 100 Mile House to Williams Lake, we admired the vistas. We really liked what we saw. We knew we wouldn't want to live there, because it would be too far from Vancouver, but we did like it a lot. We drove around in Williams Lake and found the site of the Stampede. It was now empty and looked forlorn and abandoned without horses and cowboys. We had something to eat, and continued on our way to the Dude Ranch.

Suddenly, by the side of the road, there was a person who looked like a native Indian. However, this person did not look like the Indians on the screen. This person weaved from side to side, was dressed in rags, and was not very pretty to look at. He was obviously drunk. I closed my eyes in dismay, and thought "Poor Mike. He so looked forward to seeing his first Indian." I stole a look at the boy. He was frowning and did not look very happy.

Then he said, "Well, that was not a very nice one, was it, Mom?"

"No, darling, it wasn't, but we have always known that the Indians had a problem with alcohol, remember? Karl May wrote about that too. Their systems don't seem to digest alcohol very well, and that is why they always seem to be drunk, when they may only have had one or two drinks."

Mike nodded his head. It was true. Karl May did warn about that. There must be a lot more Indians in the area; not all was lost! *Too bad,* I thought. We should have come for Stampede time. I was sure we would have seen more heroic-looking Indians then.

We duly arrived at the Dude-farm and were soon settled in our cabin. It was primitive, as expected, but rather clean so we were content. We could build a campfire in front of the cabin and barbecue our meat there. It was fun sitting around the fire, trying to listen to all the sounds around us. We had our steaks and Serge had his beer and we all felt that we were really living in the West. Then we were hailed by a man who told us he was our neighbour. He also turned out to be rather drunk, but Serge did not want to be impolite so asked him to sit down.

The man liked to talk, especially after he asked—and was given—a bottle of beer. He proceeded to tell us all about the other neighbours, about the owners, about the Indians, and by the time we were yawning with sleep we knew exactly what was going on with whom and where and why. Mikey's ears were wide-open. In the middle of all this, we were suddenly disturbed by some noises in the bush around us. There appeared two donkeys who were ready to nibble on everything in sight. We had hoped for horses, but donkeys were all right for now.

CHAPTER EIGHTY-EIGHT

In which we fall in love with the '108', meet a blue bird and a realtor and his charming family, and we are tempted to buy a house!

After we left Williams Lake, we continued to the 108 Ranch and the beautiful hotel there. It was so well situated, on a slight slope towards the gorgeous golf course, with a view of the 108 Lake, that we were quite impressed with its civility. Especially after our stay up north, I must admit, where the quality of the people we met was less than impressive. Oh, the people had been nice and kind enough; no complaints there. But they were on the whole so rough; we were used to Holland where most men still wore suits and neck ties and shiny shoes. We had to get used to COWBOY COUNTRY!

We had a lovely suite with an extra room for Mike. That night, the manager of the hotel and his wife invited us to have dinner at their place, as we had come from so far to visit them. The next morning when we got up, we saw the most beautiful little blue bird sitting on the rail, looking at us with its intelligent eyes. "Oh," Mike said. "Aunt Ruth told me that seeing blue birds means happiness. Dad, we should really buy a house here!" Serge laughed, but we did get the phone number of a good real estate agent from the manager.

The next day, we made an appointment with the agent to see some places, just to get an idea of the possibilities. Then Serge went to play golf and Mike and I went for a swim in the pool and a long sunbathe. In the afternoon we went around with the agent and saw some houses. The first ones were not great, but then he showed us a rancher with a huge basement. It had a lovely view with a nice back yard, abutting a large grassy area that went down to another lake, on which each owner was allowed to place two horses to graze on. It looked amazing to us.

Mike and I on our first Trail Ride with a new friend during our first visit to the 108 Ranch.

We were also told that there was a large arena close to that lake, with a beautiful indoor riding ring, within walking distance from the house. There was another free lot to the left of the house we were looking at, as well as another empty lot to the right. We talked it over when we were alone again, and finally decided to put in an offer on all three of the properties. After some haggling, we agreed on the price and the three properties became ours. We were lucky in that the owners of the house did not mind renting the place back from us for a year. Later, Serge built us a beautiful little barn with a long paddock; Mike was all ready to go.

CHAPTER EIGHTY-NINE

In which we find out how young this country is, and where we say good-bye to Holland—we all cry a little, but look forward to Canada.

The three of us were quite excited, as one can imagine. It was a big step to take, so far from the Netherlands, and also so far from the Middle East. Serge could be called back there at any time, while the harbour of Kuwait was being constructed. Serge was sixty-nine when we made this decision; I was actually very impressed with the fact that he still had enough adventurous spirit in him to take such a big step.

After our eventful residence at the so-called Dude Ranch, and the purchase of our new properties on the 108 Ranch, we were happy to head south again. We stopped at 100 Mile House and had some lunch at the pub. They were all in a very celebratory mood, and we asked why that was. Well, they said, the town was celebrating its tenth anniversary of existence. They were all very proud of their little town and toasted all and everyone who came into the pub. We looked at each other and smiled. We congratulated them and hoped for many, many more years. We had our lunch, then they all toasted us again and we left.

Once we were out of sight we started to laugh. This country was so young, so incredibly young! Amsterdam, the capital of Holland, was actually also celebrating something—its 800th birthday! We couldn't tell them that; they didn't need to be reminded how old Europe was. We were happy to leave them in contentment with their ten years of existence of their own little town. Which we came to love very much as well, later on.

This was what most people who heard of our plans thought—They are crazy to do it. Serge just smiled and said, "Better crazy than bored." My parents were rather shocked that we had really already bought property in British Columbia. And in cowboy country, no less. It did not take my dad long to decide that he also wanted to come to Canada to be near us. He also loved riding horses. My mom was less enthused about the plan, but had to go along with it as she also wanted to be near her daughter and grandson.

We sold our beautiful house, including the extensive wine-cellar contents; it was actually one of the big attractions of the property. We wanted to take our horse Dushka with us, but that turned out to be a very complicated thing to do. I finally managed to talk the German Olympic horse team into adding our Duschka to their own lot. They were going to fly to Montreal in Canada for the 1976 Summer Olympics. I was obliged to first send a blood sample from Dushka, because the Canadians didn't want to risk to have equine infectious anemia brought into the country.

There was another very important reason why we had finally decided to go to Canada. The school system in Holland in those days was not very nice in our eyes. No matter what the numbers said in the report cards of the last year in high school, it did not matter. To enter university all you had to do was put your name in the hat, show your high school diploma, and with luck they would pick your name to enter your chosen curriculum. We had heard of a case where a very brilliant young woman had put her name in three years in a row never to get chosen. She wanted to be a scientist. Michael wanted to be a veterinarian. It was hard to get in, and in this case, he could have been rejected for years in a row. We thought to avoid this by having him study in Canada.

I was sad to say goodbye to our good friends in Holland. It was also difficult to say goodbye to our tennis club. We had just celebrated our fifth anniversary with great fanfare. But, the Canadian adventure beckoned, and we could not look back; it was the future that was important.

CANADA, HERE WE COME!

EPILOGUE

The first forty years have been covered, but the next forty or so years would need another book. Unfortunately, I don't know how many good years I still have ahead of me, so I will, for now, just give the bare outlines of our years in our beautiful new country, Canada.

We took a boat to Montreal and then stayed a few days, because we had to get the result of Dushka's blood test. We found the place, and then had terrible news; Dushka was a carrier of the disease. She was not allowed into the country… Mike and I cried for days; we so loved that horse. Serge felt awful; he just wanted to see us happy, and this was hard for him to take. I had a lot of work ahead of me, undoing all the arrangements with the German Equestrian team and we now had to sell our beloved Dushka.

We next took the train to Vancouver, and what a trip that was! We had games and books with us, to while away boring hours, but there were none. We were all glued to the windows, admiring everything we saw. Canada is such a vast country; it was unbelievable to us that we had to travel by train for four days before reaching the other end. (*In Holland it takes about two hours!*).

We managed to buy a car in Vancouver and left the next day to take possession of our new house. We were so happy to be there, and Mike had a very interesting time, learning to be a cowboy. He had bought a real cowboy hat in Vancouver, but the first thing the cowboys did was demolish his hat! A cowboy hat had to be creased and dirty and well-used before it could be considered a real cowboy hat. We started learning the cowboy ways!

We took Mike to the high school in 100 Mile House and talked with the principal. He asked Mike what subjects he had had in his last year in Holland. Mike told him. Then the principal asked him, "What about languages; did you learn any there?"

"Yes," said Mike, "I had to learn six languages."

The principal stared at him. "Six languages? What could they be?"

Mike answered, "English, Dutch, French, German, Greek, and Latin."

The principal looked at us, spread his arms wide and said, "Well, you tell me what grade you want to go into; we can't compete with such a curriculum."

Mike decided to go into the class that was suitable for his age, and has never regretted it. The school had some really good teachers, especially in math, and Mike had a good time in the school. Yes, there were struggles with the other students in the beginning, but that is food for another book.

The first part of our stay in B.C. was dedicated to owning horses. I bred racehorses (without a great deal of success, I must confess), and Mike rode in the three-day events. I got very involved and created such events at the 108 Ranch. When

Mike was twenty, he won the individual bronze medal for the North-American Young Riders Three-Day Event competition in Chicago with his horse Othello and his team won gold. Still a highlight in his career.

Michael and Othello going cross country in Chicago.

Serge played a lot of golf, and he even started to learn cross-country skiing. He kept himself busy with all kinds of things, and was really happy in Canada. He did have to go back to Kuwait once or twice, but he did it without suffering ill-effects from the long trip. I became involved with a Mennonite Church, became a Born-Again Christian, and involved the rest of the family as well. It became a very important thing for all of us.

Little Janine came to visit us every two years for at least a month. She and Mike went in canoes on the lake, went fishing and swimming, and they climbed on their horses as often as they could. One day she decided to stay; she still wanted to marry her Mikey. He thought of her as his sister, but that changed one day. They have been married for over thirty-two years now; they really have known each other a whole lifetime. They have four children (a boy and three girls) and now have five grandchildren; two of them red-headed like their mom and like my dad—he would have been so proud.

Mike, Janine, Olivia, Robyn, and Alex with their beautiful Golden Retrievers Bella and Beau. Number 4, lovely daughter Naomi, was a very happy surprise much later.

My mother died of her fifth stroke when she was sixty-seven years old; a very sad loss. My dad found another lady to be his traveling companion and friend. He died of Alzheimer's when he was eighty-six. Serge died of kidney failure when he was eighty-five; I was fifty-six at the time.

After Serge died, I went to university to get my bachelor's degree. I majored in English literature with an extended minor in psychology and took many courses in history and archaeology.

Then I discovered the Society for Learning in Retirement (a charitable society) in Kelowna, where Mike had his veterinary practice. I soon started to lead classes in ancient civilizations. I did that for sixteen years and loved every minute of it. I usually had thirty or more people in my class, which was great. It felt so good to be able to share my passion for those ancient civilizations with all those like-minded folks. I quit when I was eighty-two because of troubles with eyes and ears. I made many wonderful friends, whom I treasure.

I even found another man to love twelve years ago. I was seventy-two years old when I met him. A friend had persuaded me to go to a singles dance. I said no, of course. Who would want to ask someone of my age to dance? She was very persuasive, so I finally decided to try it out. I actually danced quite a bit that first night, and decided to go back again.

That night there had been a good frost. As soon as I arrived at the dance hall and stepped out of my car, I felt that I stood on an ice patch. I was wearing my high heels and did not dare to move. It was dark, and I could not see anyone else. What should I do? Then, out of the corner of my eye, I saw a vague shadow move. I called out, "Hello there, I need help!"

A man walked towards me and he said, "What is the problem?" I explained the situation. He laughed, grabbed me under his arm, and he never let go. That was twelve years ago. We fell very much in love to my utter amazement. I had no idea that people of that age could still feel that way. His name is Henry Fast. He is tall and still a very good-looking man. Lucky me!

Henry and I ready to go to a New-Year's eve party.

We did not get married as we were both rather set in our ways, but I spend one week at his place and one week at my own place where I see a lot of my kids. It works quite well, and in our old age we manage to laugh a lot about our age-related shortcomings these days. He even managed to take all my classes during those twelve years, as he is quite interested in history as well. I consider myself very lucky to have found love twice in my life.

Religion has always been a problem for me, and being a Born-Again Christian could not last. There were too many things that just did not make sense. I did believe in Jesus and all the good things he taught us, but I had great difficulty in believing in the God of the old Testament. He was not a God of love, but a very cruel God. I am sorry if I hurt people's feelings, saying this, but it is <u>my</u> life, and this has been <u>my</u> struggle. I always felt a need to pray, but to whom?

In the end, I had an epiphany. I was sitting outside late in the afternoon on a beautiful spring day. The sun was still warming my face and I felt at peace with the world. Suddenly, I had the feeling that everything became intensified, I felt everything almost exploding with life and sweetness. I could sense every blade of grass growing towards the ultimate light up above. And I knew that God is Nature; maybe God is the brains of nature. God and nature are one. Nature is everywhere and in everything, not just in this universe, but in all others—no matter how far away they are. Only God can be that big.

It was a great experience, and it has brought me solace in my struggle for finding the truth of who I am, why I am here, and what the purpose is for me in this life. I am here to hone my soul, as my son likes to say, and I agree with him. Every struggle life throws at us is there in order to teach us to overcome. But above all, I am here to love. To love my neighbor, no matter what color or inclination, to spread love around as much as possible. Love for people, animals, or even situations. I failed many, many times, but that is all right; I also succeeded many times, and that is good.

The God I have found lives in my heart, in yours, and in everyone's heart. We are all connected by this great bond, people and animals alike. God is everywhere, as Nature is everywhere, and we are all part of this great, wonderful empire, attached to each other by Nature's strings.

Alexander Pope said it so beautifully a long time ago, as I just discovered:

All are but one stupendous Whole
*** Whose body Nature is, and God the Soul.***

This is the story in a nutshell of our years in Canada. I learned a great deal. All of us learned a great deal. We love this beautiful country, and believe that it is one of the very best places in the world to live.

THE END

Printed in Canada